The Old-Time, Blue-Ribbon Gardener's Handbook

The Old-Time, Blue-Ribbon Gardener's Handbook

TIPS, TECHNIQUES, AND PROJECTS

Susan Waggoner

RIZZOLI
NEW YORK

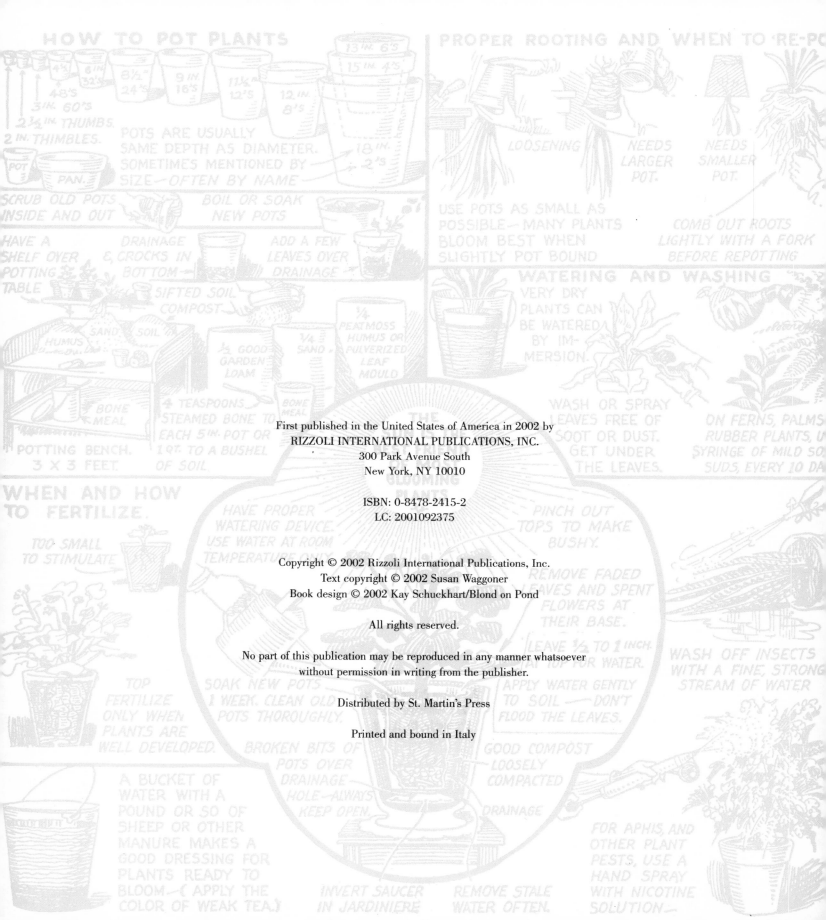

First published in the United States of America in 2002 by
RIZZOLI INTERNATIONAL PUBLICATIONS, INC.
300 Park Avenue South
New York, NY 10010

ISBN: 0-8478-2415-2
LC: 2001092375

Distributed by St. Martin's Press

Printed and bound in Italy

Contents

"This is an age of simplicity," *Better Homes and Gardens* magazine proclaimed in September of 1935. "Simple lines in gardens as well as in swimsuits, furniture, and architecture." An update on the ornate Victorian yard, the redesigned garden for the "New American" home still found room for such attractions as a front lawn, living room terrace, garden terrace, pleasure lawn, wading pool, playhouse, toolhouse, hospitality room, dunking

THE WELL-PLANNED *Garden*

tank (no word on who or what was to be dunked), and small vegetable plot, charmingly referred to as a Sandwich-and-Appetizer Garden.

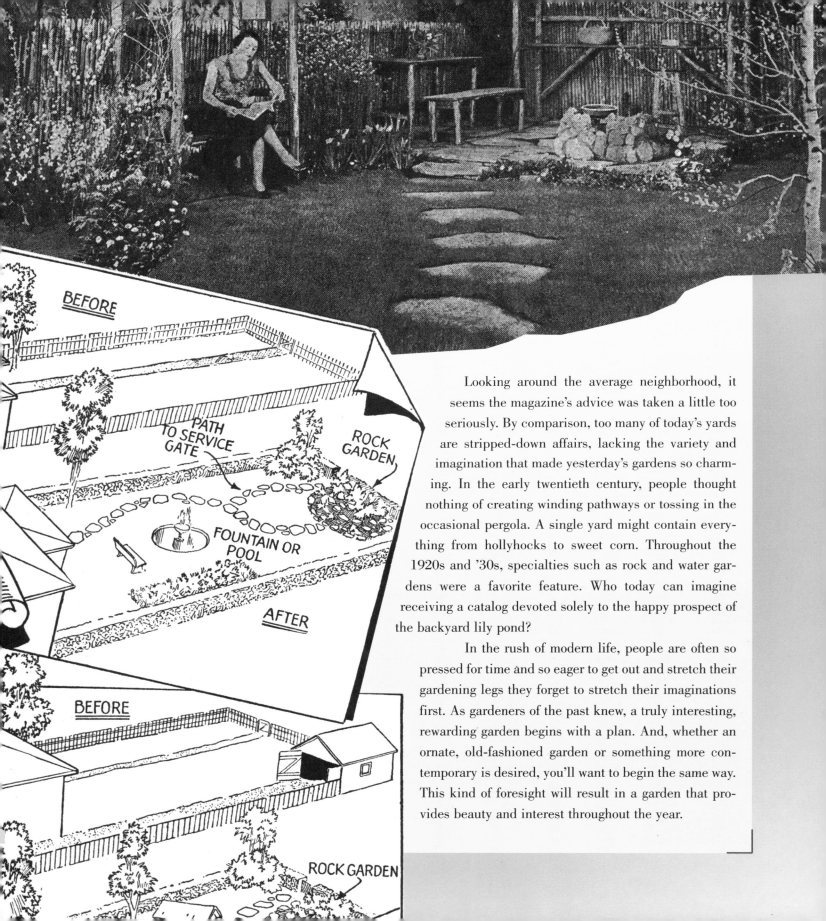

BEFORE

PATH
TO SERVICE
GATE

ROCK
GARDEN

FOUNTAIN OR
POOL

AFTER

BEFORE

ROCK GARDEN

Looking around the average neighborhood, it seems the magazine's advice was taken a little too seriously. By comparison, too many of today's yards are stripped-down affairs, lacking the variety and imagination that made yesterday's gardens so charming. In the early twentieth century, people thought nothing of creating winding pathways or tossing in the occasional pergola. A single yard might contain everything from hollyhocks to sweet corn. Throughout the 1920s and '30s, specialties such as rock and water gardens were a favorite feature. Who today can imagine receiving a catalog devoted solely to the happy prospect of the backyard lily pond?

In the rush of modern life, people are often so pressed for time and so eager to get out and stretch their gardening legs they forget to stretch their imaginations first. As gardeners of the past knew, a truly interesting, rewarding garden begins with a plan. And, whether an ornate, old-fashioned garden or something more contemporary is desired, you'll want to begin the same way. This kind of foresight will result in a garden that provides beauty and interest throughout the year.

HOW TO MAKE A GARDEN PLAN

Making a garden plan is easy, fun, and inexpensive. You will need:

1. graph paper (sheets with eight to ten squares per inch work best)
2. pencils and erasers
3. 12" ruler
4. scissors

First, create a scale drawing of your house and lot. To do this, you will need to know the measurements of each and be able to accurately place your house on the lot. Decide what scale to use (such as 2 squares = 1 foot) and, with the ruler, outline your house and the boundaries of your lot. If your drawing won't fit on a single page, use tape to join additional pages, making sure to keep the graphed squares in alignment.

Once you have drawn your house and lot, add the other "immovables"—large, semi-permanent features that you have no current plans to change, such as the driveway, sidewalk, fence, deck, patio, swimming pool, and large trees, shrubs, and plant beds. If your lot is on a rise or includes slopes or terraces, you will also want to use hash marks to show where elevation changes begin and where they end.

You now have a basic canvas on which to work. Before you begin marking it up, prepare several more just like it, so you can start over on clean sheets if a particular plan doesn't work out and develop different plans for each season. (You can let a photocopier do the work for you or, if you have a computer and scanner, keep a master on disk.)

Now you're ready for the fun part. Sit back, put your feet up, and dream. Think of some of the things you want your garden to achieve. Do you want to screen out unattractive views? Ensure privacy? Raise your own fruits or vegetables?

NEIGHBORS SHARE A POOL BUILT BETWEEN THEIR LOTS

WATER INLET

WATER LINE

$1\frac{1}{2}$" DRAIN PIPE IS UNSCREWED TO DRAIN POOL

SCREEN

CROWN OF PLANT SET EVEN WITH SURFACE OF SOIL

SAND SOIL

BRASS COUPLING

24"

6" CONCRETE

10" EXPANSION COURSE

REINFORCING RODS OR WIRE NET

TUB SET UP ON STONES TO BRING

CINDERS

DETAIL OF POOL CONSTRUCTION & LILY POND

Create a small, spirit-soothing oasis, a place for your children to play, or a cutting garden that will supply you with fresh flowers? Don't be afraid to put more than one thing on your wish list—the purpose of developing a plan is to incorporate as many desirable features as possible without creating garden chaos.

With your wish list in mind, begin considering specific features you might want to include. In *The Complete Book of Garden Magic*, originally published in 1935, Roy Biles listed the most popular garden attractions of the era. They're still a good way to get the imagination flowing:

PLANT INTEREST		UTILITY FEATURES		ORNAMENTAL	
Open Lawn	Rock Garden	Garden or Tea House	Vegetable Garden	Fences	Bird Baths
Foundation Planting	Water Garden			Trellis	Fountains
	Vines	Outdoor Living Room	Cold Frame	Gates	Miniature Gardens
Perennials	Flowering			Seats	
Annuals	Shrubbery:	Play Yard		Walks	Mirror Pool
Dahlias	(a) Fruit	Drying Yard		Steps	Bird Houses
Irises	(b) Shade	Terraces		Vases	
Bulbs	(c) Grove	Service Plot		Statuary	
Rose Garden	(d) Specimen	Green House		Sun Dials	
Climbing Roses	(e) Flowering	Propagating Bed		Globes	

At this point, it will be helpful to draw outlines of your desired features on a separate sheet of paper or cardboard, using the same scale used to create your basic canvas. Label each template clearly, shading the edges or using colored pencils to add definition. Cut the pieces and begin experimenting by arranging them on your canvas. As you do this, don't forget to walk around your house and yard (see illustration on page 15). Try to visualize different features, both as they will appear outside and as you look at them from your windows. An old gardener's trick is to use a garden hose as a stand-in for projected borders. This can be especially helpful for planning asymmetrical features such as meandering paths and flower beds with irregular borders.

DESIGN POINTERS

When finalizing your garden design, there are many factors to consider. Keeping a few principles in mind will help you achieve success and avoid disappointment.

- Create a plan that fits your lot comfortably. Allow ample space between features rather than packing them in.
- If your lot is long and narrow, keep side borders narrow and use the rear for special features.
- If your lot is short and wide, use wider borders at the side (such as a lilac hedge) and keep rear borders shallow.
- Keep your plan balanced. Draw a line down the middle of your property from front to back. A wide expanse of lawn on one side should have an approximately equal amount on the opposite.
- Avoid symmetry. While your plan should be balanced, one side should not be a mirror image of the other. A balanced but irregular plan will add interest and make your yard seem bigger.

- Remember that trees, flower beds, and other large features placed in the center of your lawn break up the view and make the area seem smaller. Wherever possible, keep center vistas uncluttered and use these features to frame or accent the sweep of lawn.
- Try to position flower beds and fruit and vegetable gardens where they will get the necessary sun, and away from large trees and other plants that will compete for food and moisture.
- Think about whether you want a formal or informal plan. If you want both, separate them into distinct features. For example, a formal cutting garden or rose garden works well with an informal overall plan.

FORMAL OR INFORMAL GARDEN?

The generally informal plan requires much less upkeep, less strict attention to detail of design. However, the plantings must be good as the interest centers on them rather than the design. With the formal or semiformal plan the emphasis is on the design and mass effect of the plantings rather than on individual specimens. Where growing conditions are good the informal or semiformal style usually gives the most satisfaction.

—The Complete Book of Garden Magic, 1935

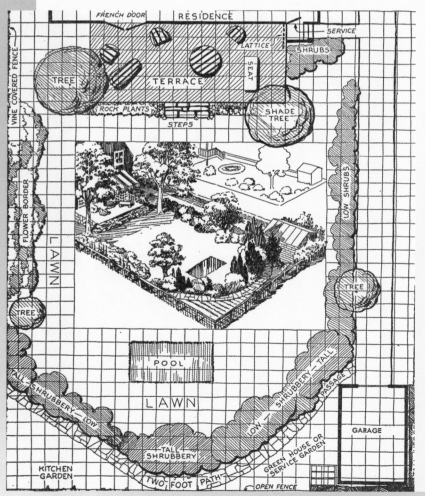

While it's certainly true that informal gardens are less demanding than formal ones, and complement the casual style of suburban living, don't dismiss the possibility of including some formal elements in your own garden, such as a geometric layout, pools, paths, and structured borders. Carefully thought out and correctly placed, they can distinguish an otherwise ordinary yard by providing a focal point that adds both unity and interest. You needn't do your whole yard on this grand scale, but reserving a nook, a corner, or even a single bed for experimentation can be a rewarding adventure. And, as the sample plans to the right show, a formal bed or area can take almost any shape your imagination desires.

CHOOSING PLANTS

Once you have an idea of the features you want and where they'll go, you're ready to think about choosing specific plant varieties. Here's where the present is definitely better than the past, as many species now have specially bred varieties tailored for particular climates. Your choices are wider than ever, but here are some things to keep in mind:

- Use "four season" thinking. What will go in that flower bed after the spring tulips fade? How will your garden look in winter? Make a separate plan for every season of the year.

- Start with less expensive, easy-to-grow varieties. This allows you to "test drive" your plan as you gain experience.

- Beware of plants from far-away places. Plants that flourish in a distant climate or require a specialized soil mix may not thrive under local conditions.

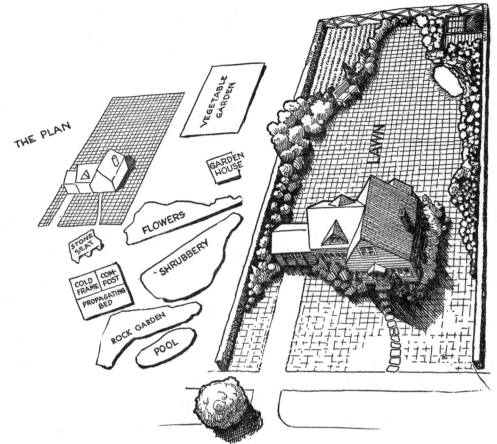

- In spacing new shrubs, remember that they will grow considerably in just a few years. If you are concerned about bare spots in borders and hedges, fill the gaps with temporary plantings that can be eliminated as the shrubs fill out.

- Note sun patterns. Use densely shaded areas for recreation or open lawn, and choose plants that require less sun for semi-shaded areas.

- Transplanting large trees or shrubs can be a problem, as shock can weaken the plant and cause it to stop growing. A smaller plant, carefully tended, will give better results in less time.

- Think about height. In border plantings (plantings that abut a fence, walkway, property line, or some other feature) and foundation plantings (those directly abutting the house and garage) keep the tallest plants to the back and shortest plants to the front, closest to the viewer's eye.

- Choose plants that harmonize with each other, not only in color, but in size, texture, foliage, growing requirements, and even scent. Study your planting lists carefully to orchestrate a succession of blooms in your flower beds, and to ensure that plants will not be competing with each other for light and space.

Make a note of any changes you make to your plan after actual planting begins. It's also a good idea to date the plan and, as the season progresses, keep track of developments. In this way, you will have a record to work from in future seasons—the beginning of a gardener's notebook.

Good garden work needs good tools and materials but we do not advise rushing into quantity purchases without careful consideration. First have a place to keep them, or if you have them, get them clean and sharp. Perfection was never achieved in a minute.

—The Complete Book of Garden Magic, 1935

THE RIGHT *Tools*

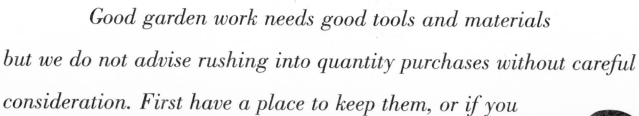

Garden gadgets seem to multiply exponentially with each passing season. But it's not necessarily true that more tools make for a better garden—or a better

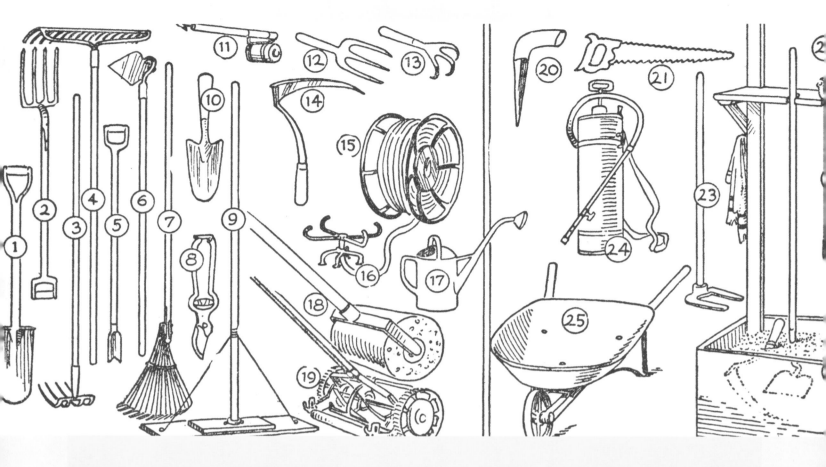

gardener, for that matter. Most of the tools that worked in the past are still top-of-the-list today, although you might want to replace the old-style rotary mower with a power model!

How much equipment you need, of course, depends on the size and diversity of your garden, available storage space, and how much you want to spend. Like great chefs, great gardeners can often get by with a few simple tools. If you don't want to invest in a lot of equipment, start with a core group that includes a shovel, rake, garden hose, sprinkler, sprinkling can, mower, hand cultivator, trowel, and all-purpose shears.

1. **PLANTING SHOVEL:** Small and very handy for digging.

2. **SPADING OR DIGGING FORK:** Easier to wield than a spade and excellent for breaking up soil.

3. **CULTIVATOR:** Ideal for keeping flower beds in shape.

4. **HOE RAKE:** Removes debris from the lawn and can be used instead of the cultivator.

5. **WEED SPUD:** Removes surface-rooting weeds such as dock and plantain.

6. **HOE:** A must for anyone with flower or vegetable beds. Good for shallow cultivation and digging shallow trenches for seeds and seedlings.

7. **BROOM RAKE:** Use to remove rubbish such as fallen leaves and litter from the lawn.

8. **SHEARS:** The size depends on the purpose. Short-handled shears are fine for most pruning jobs, but long-handled shears are a good investment if you have tall shrubs and trees.

9. **HOMEMADE TAMPER:** It's well worth the time to fashion one from an old broom handle and a length of board. They are excellent for eliminating air pockets from recently dug soil.

10. **TROWEL:** For hand digging, and especially useful for planting flowers and bulbs.

11. **HAND SPRAYER:** From the days when DDT was legal. It's still useful if you mix your own insect remedies but if you buy premixed products, this isn't necessary.

12. **HAND FORK:** Allows "surgical strike" digging in a small area.

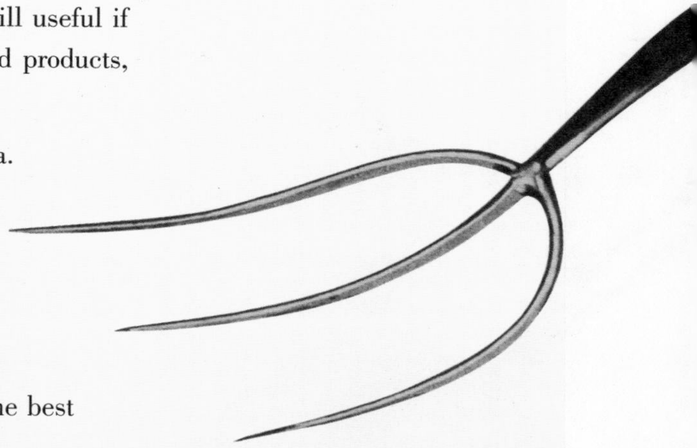

13. **HAND CULTIVATOR:** Another "indispensable" for hand-to-hand encounters with the soil, this tool is great for breaking up soil in small areas.

14. **SICKLE:** A very, very early forerunner of the weed whacker.

15. **GARDEN HOSE:** Impossible to improve on, and still one of the best gardening tools of all time.

16. **SPRINKLER:** Every gardener needs at least one.

17. **SPRINKLING CAN:** A hose can't take the place of this tool. During dry spells, it lets you gently bathe flowers and foliage. It's also handy for mixing and dispensing soluble plant food.

18. **ROLLER:** A worthwhile investment for anyone with a good-sized lawn. Used for firming freshly planted soil and sod.

19. **LAWN MOWER:** There's nothing like the sound of a hand-powered mower—but modern power mowers are much easier to push.

20. **DIBBLE:** Used for planting seeds and seedlings. Just punch down to the depth desired and you're ready to plant.

21. **PRUNING SAW:** Unless you have large branches to prune or remove, you won't need this.

22. **SHELF-TYPE RACK:** Allows you to hang tools up and out of the way. It not only saves space but preserves blades and working edges by keeping them off the ground.

23. **POTATO HOE:** Good for deep cultivation and a must if you grow spuds.

24. **KNAPSACK SPRAYER:** Since today's insecticides and weed-killers usually come in their own application containers, you can delete this one from your shopping list.

25. **WHEELBARROW:** An excellent investment, provided you have a place to store it. No matter how small your lawn is, there's always something to haul from one place to another.

26. **BOX OF SAND:** See instructions for making your own under "Tool Upkeep," below.

27. **LAWN EDGER:** Before today's mechanical gadgets, people used these to trim grass along sidewalks and driveways. Clippers work better, and are a worthwhile purchase.

TOOL UPKEEP

When choosing tools, buy the best quality you can afford. And, once purchased, keep tools in good condition. This means keeping them in a waterproof shed or garage, or even bringing them inside if no other shelter is available.

A rack with a box of sand, as shown in the illustration on page 18, is ideal for all bladed tools. You can construct this yourself, either as a one-piece unit or as a box (measuring at least twelve inches deep and long enough to accommodate your tools) which can be placed beneath a rack. Remember to mount the rack at a height that allows the blade ends of the tools to dip into the box. Once you have the box, fill it with coarse sand that has been thoroughly dried in the sun. Then gradually mix in clean oil, adding just enough to give the sand a slightly oily feeling. If the tool ends appear greasy and slippery, you have added too much oil and need to mix in more dry sand. Storing tools in this way keeps them from rusting, and the invisible layer of oil makes for easy cleaning after use. Hand tools can also be stored in this way—just remember to keep working parts free of the sand. If you are storing shears, submerge only the blades, and make sure the pivot is kept clean. It is a good idea to wipe tools with a cloth before using them, and to clean them again, first with a lightly oiled rag and then with a dry cloth, before putting them away.

If tools need a "tune-up," first soak them in water and scrub them well. Then, clean metal parts with a wire brush or fine emery paper. If blades are rusty, apply a commercial rust remover. If wooden handles have splinters or peeling paint, sand them down and then repaint them with a bright color such as red or yellow. Now the tools will be easier to spot when left outside.

Of all the tools in the garden, none is as essential—or abused—as the garden hose. Every year, millions of them are run over with lawn mowers and wheelbarrows, abandoned in the hot sun, or tossed in the garage with kinks and knots in their lengths. When not in use, hoses should be stored in the shade. They should be on a reel or in a loose, tangle-free coil. When storing the hose for the winter, make sure all the water has been drained from it.

A little care will keep tools in good condition for years. Instead of spending money on replacements, you can buy new plants for your garden.

HEDGE SHEARS
10 Inch Blade

You'll want these fine shears for pruning hedges and shrubs. See Page 4 for other pruning equipment.

3 PIECE GARDEN SET

It's easy to garden with this small size, light weight rake, hoe and spade. Turn to page 14 for other handy lawn and garden tools.

3½ Gallon
COMPRESSED AIR SPRAYER

Does a powerful job spraying trees, flowers and vegetables. See Page 17 for further details & other models.

SPECIALIZED TOOLS

Depending on what type of gardening you do, you may want to acquire specialized tools beyond the basics described on the previous page. These can be worthwhile, labor-saving investments—just research brands and best buys first, and resist the urge to purchase every shiny new toy you see in the catalogs!

Much labor can be saved with proper tools. The dandelion rake easily takes off blossoms before they bloom without injuring grass roots. A lawn fertilizer spreader does hours of work in a few minutes. A grass whip, swung like a golf club, trims weeds under fences and close to walls without stooping and with little effort. A floral spade or foot trowel, with five-by-seven-inch blade, can be used as a garden walking stick and is always handy for a multitude of garden tasks.

—*The Complete Book of Garden Magic*, 1935

In addition to tools specifically for the garden, don't forget the usefulness of some common household items such as a stable stepladder; ball of twine; bucket; kneeling pad; waterproof marker; and cloths for wiping off tools.

Eclipse HAND MOWERS

Vital Distinctions

COMPARE!

Before buying another standard type mower, match an Eclipse against the field. Think of Eclipse from the standpoint of cutting expenses. Finger Tip Adjustment saves annual adjusting and sharpening bills. Think of Eclipse as always sharp, from the first mowing of the year to the last. No Mower is better able to stand comparison than Eclipse. See it, then decide.

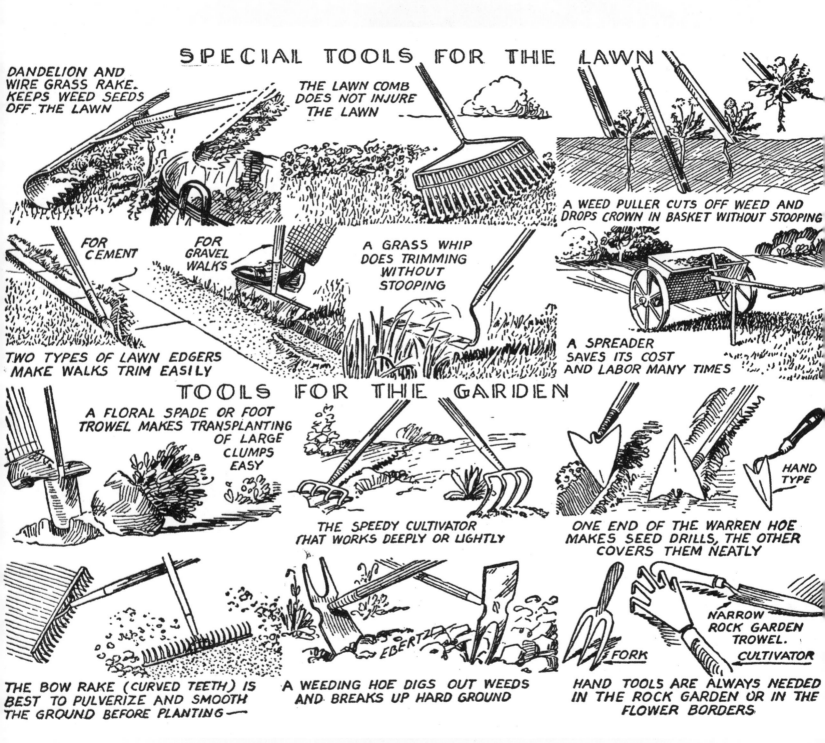

SPECIAL TOOLS FOR THE LAWN

DANDELION AND WIRE GRASS RAKE. KEEPS WEED SEEDS OFF THE LAWN

THE LAWN COMB DOES NOT INJURE THE LAWN

A WEED PULLER CUTS OFF WEED AND DROPS CROWN IN BASKET WITHOUT STOOPING

FOR CEMENT

FOR GRAVEL WALKS

A GRASS WHIP DOES TRIMMING WITHOUT STOOPING

TWO TYPES OF LAWN EDGERS MAKE WALKS TRIM EASILY

A SPREADER SAVES ITS COST AND LABOR MANY TIMES

TOOLS FOR THE GARDEN

A FLORAL SPADE OR FOOT TROWEL MAKES TRANSPLANTING OF LARGE CLUMPS EASY

THE SPEEDY CULTIVATOR THAT WORKS DEEPLY OR LIGHTLY

ONE END OF THE WARREN HOE MAKES SEED DRILLS, THE OTHER COVERS THEM NEATLY

HAND TYPE

THE BOW RAKE (CURVED TEETH) IS BEST TO PULVERIZE AND SMOOTH THE GROUND BEFORE PLANTING —

A WEEDING HOE DIGS OUT WEEDS AND BREAKS UP HARD GROUND

EBERTZ

FORK

NARROW ROCK GARDEN TROWEL.

CULTIVATOR

HAND TOOLS ARE ALWAYS NEEDED IN THE ROCK GARDEN OR IN THE FLOWER BORDERS

23

Soil THE KEY INGREDIENT

Soil is the single most important ingredient in gardens. While all soil is composed of finely ground bits of rock and humus (decaying vegetable debris), the mix and chemical composition of these ingredients vary widely. Some soils retain more water than others, some are denser than others, and some are richer—or poorer—in the nutrients that nourish plants. Even experienced gardeners sometimes overlook soil as a crucial factor in planning and planting, or believe that adding fertilizer and a little topsoil is an all-purpose compensator.

During World War II, gardening assumed an importance it hadn't enjoyed since pioneer days. Victory gardens—designed to raise vegetables for the home so commercial supplies could go to troops overseas—sprang up all over America, and a good crop meant the difference between eating well and struggling along on ration coupons. During the war years, *The Home Garden* magazine devoted many articles to the all-important topic of dirt. The same properties it ascribed to ideal soil back then hold true today.

Soil should contain an adequate supply of nutrient materials, it should be well supplied with humus, it should be porous enough to permit the free passage of air and water, and yet compact enough to provide a firm anchorage for roots. It should also be well-drained . . . but at the same time it should be sufficiently retentive of moisture for the plants not to suffer unduly during dry periods. And, finally, the deeper the layer of topsoil that is in nearly ideal condition for root growth, the better.

—*The Home Garden*, March 1945

Two or three gardeners may be gifted with this ideal blend, but who's ever met these lucky souls? Most people have to do the best they can with the soil fate has put them in charge of. To make the most of your soil, it is important to know its structure and composition, improve it when possible, tend it according to its needs, and select the plants best suited for it.

Good garden loam is made up of 40% clay, 40% vegetable matter, and 20% sand.

—*America's Garden Book*, 1939

SOIL TYPE

The ideal soil is a rich blend of sand, clay, and humus. This highly desirable "common" garden loam isn't common at all, and many people have soil that either contains too much clay or is too sandy.

Clay soils are good at holding water, but this makes them heavy, slow to dry out, and slow to warm in the spring. If clay soil is left untended after a rain, it may form a hard crust as it dries (think of clay tiles, baked in a kiln). The crust prevents air and moisture from filtering through the soil and this leaves plant roots inadequately nourished. The remedy for this is to turn up the soil while it is still wet. However, working with the soil when it is too wet will cause it to form clumps which, when dry, are difficult to break up. The gardener with clay soil must not only learn how to work the soil, but when to work it. In general, clay soil is more difficult to manage than other soil types, and requires more active maintenance.

Sandy soils, unlike clay soils, are quite porous. They are well aerated, quick to warm in the spring, and easy to work. The obvious drawback is that these soils do not retain water, and applications of food and fertilizer are often leached away. The main challenge for gardeners with sandy soil is to make sure their plants receive adequate nutrients.

Gardeners dealing with very sandy soils or clay-heavy mixes will want to improve the soil structure of plant beds and gardens whenever possible.

- **TO IMPROVE CLAY SOIL:** Add sand and humus to lighten the soil and improve its nutrient content. It is also a good idea to spade the soil in the fall and leave it somewhat rough—winter frost will make clumps easier to break up when spring arrives.
- **TO IMPROVE SANDY SOIL:** A liberal addition of humus will improve nutrient values and increase water retention. Because humus is organic matter that decomposes over time, and because nutrients are washed away with each rain, additional organic material will have to be added occasionally.

Effective, easy-to-obtain sources of humus include compost, peat moss, shredded leaves, and leaf mold (fallen leaves that have been composted for at least six months).

—The Complete Book of Garden Magic, 1935

SOIL TESTING

In addition to knowing what type of soil you have, it's also important to know what nutrients your soil may be lacking. Fortunately, most states have departments of agriculture that will test your soil for you, just as they did fifty years ago. You can find them by contacting your County Extension office. If your state does not have this service, local nurseries or state universities can point you in the right direction. Even if you must send your samples to a private lab, the cost is usually modest and well worth the investment.

How useful the results of a soil analysis are depends, in large part, on the quality of the samples taken. Here are a few ways to take representative samples.

- Sample during the early spring or late fall. The worst time to sample is during the growing season, as plant activity and summer rains affect the soil composition.
- Take the sample from top to root level. This avoids the problem of sampling only a thin topsoil layer that may not be wholly representative. When sampling a lawn area, only go down three to six inches; when sampling an area where there will be plants, dig six to eight inches down.
- Sample correctly. Use a trowel to make an initial hole, then brush away the loose dirt. When the hole is clean, cut a thin, top-to-bottom slice from the side, just as if you were cutting a slice of cake.

- Prepare samples carefully. Spread the dirt out on a clean sheet of paper and allow it to dry thoroughly. Keep it away from other soil, dust, pesticides, fertilizer, and fumes so it doesn't become contaminated. When the soil is thoroughly dry, it can be packed for shipment. (An unused zip-style freezer bag is ideal for this purpose. Just make sure the inside of the bag is clean and dry before adding your sample.)
- Take more than one sample. Soil can vary from area to area even on a relatively small lot. Carefully label each sample taken and keep a record of what you've done.
- Sample regularly. Soil that you have cultivated and fertilized over a period of years can change, and the analysis that was accurate several years ago may no longer be helpful.

—adapted from *America's Garden Book*, 1939

SOIL FERTILITY

Soil fertility results from the interaction of a number of factors. Key them are food elements, the nutrients available to plants rooted in the soil. Once you've had your soil analyzed, you'll know which nutrients it has in abundance and which it lacks.

Today, plants need the same three nutrients to thrive—nitrogen, phosphorus, and potassium (potash)—that plants needed fifty, 500, and 5,000 years ago. While many marvelous hybrids have been created, no horticulturist has yet devised the flower, bulb, or blade of grass that can exist on nothing at all. And, for the most part, the remedies for improving soil deficiencies have not changed much over the decades, except that fertilizer today is more likely to be a concentrated chemical preparation than manure scooped up from the cow barn. In addition to nitrogen, phosphorus, and potassium, today's commercial fertilizers are also good sources of trace nutrients such as boron, copper, and iron.

- **NITROGEN** is familiar to most of us as the element that promotes the most visible plant growth, causing stems to shoot up and leaves to proliferate. Nitrogen deficiency is easily remedied with fertilizer. Since synthetic fertilizers come in different ratios of nitrogen, phosphorus, and potassium (denoted in that order by the familiar "15-30-15" or "30-10-10" numbers), your local nursery can help you choose the right mix for your soil and the plants you want to grow. If you add fertilizer, take care not to over-fertilize. Who hasn't seen tall, leggy plants that have been weakened by over-feeding? Occasionally, even untreated soil can contain too much nitrogen. If this is the case, don't add fertilizer and water frequently to deplete the abundance of this essential element.

COMPLETE FERTILITY

LOCATION — HUMUS — MOISTURE — DRAINAGE — BACTERIA — FOOD ELEMENTS

FOOD ELEMENTS

NITROGEN MAKES LEAF AND GREEN STEM GROWTH. WHEN USED IN EXCESS THE PLANTS BECOME "LEGGY" — WHILE A DEFICIENCY OF NITROGEN CONTENT MAKES WEAK, STUNTED AND WILTED PLANTS

NITROGEN

45% NITROGEN — SYNTHETIC NITROGEN

20% NITROGEN — SULPHATE OF AMMONIA

16% NITROGEN — NITRATE OF SODA

5% NITROGEN — DRIED BLOOD

5/10% NITROGEN — MANURE

RELATIVE PERCENTAGES OF NITROGEN IN DIFFERENT FERTILIZERS

HOW PLANTS ARE FED

CARBON AND OXYGEN TAKEN FROM AIR

PART OF SOLUTION EVAPORATES LEAVING FOOD ELEMENTS

PLANTS ARE COMPOSED OF 60% TO 95% WATER

FOOD SOLUTION RISES IN STEM

SOIL CONDITIONED TO HOLD WATER PROPERLY WHICH PERMITS A STEADY SUPPLY OF A WEAK FOOD SOLUTION

POTASH

(POTASSIUM) MAKES ACTIVE HEALTHY GROWTH

50% POTASH — MURIATE AND SULPHATE OF POTASH

5% POTASH — WOOD ASHES

4/10% POTASH — MANURE

PHOSPHORUS

(PHOSPHATES) MAKES STRENGTH, ROOTS, FLOWERS AND FRUITS

20% PHOSPHATE — SUPER PHOSPHATE

25% PHOSPHATE — BONE MEAL

MANURE 3/10%

FOOD ELEMENTS ARE USELESS, UNLESS IN SOLUTION AND AVAILABLE FOR PLANT USE

- **PHOSPHORUS** strengthens the plant's root system and helps it produce fully mature flowers, fruits, and vegetables. If soil is low in phosphorus, add bone meal or super phosphate (both available at garden centers) to bring levels up. If soil has too much phosphorus, choose a fertilizer that is lower in this element, keeping in mind that phosphorus is the middle number of the ratio on the package label. Planting densely will also help use up the excess.
- **POTASSIUM**, like phosphorus, strengthens roots, stems, and stalks and aids vegetable production. If soil is lacking in this element, adding soluble potash raises the levels. If soil has too much potassium, add no more until the levels fall to normal. Keep in mind that any commercial fertilizer you use will have some potassium in it, so choose one with a low ratio, the third number on the package label.

Planted in washed sand, fed with selected plant nutrients dissolved in distilled water, the growth of these plants is an accurate check on the importance of the 11 different food elements all growing things need. The test, made at a famous university, shows that lack of any of the 11 needed elements results in stunted development.

THE DIFFERENCE BETWEEN
MEDIOCRE AND *gorgeous gardens*

It can be lack of just one food element

MANURE: NATURE'S FIRST FERTILIZER

Long before today's commercial fertilizers arrived on the scene, people discovered the usefulness of animal manures. Today, animal manure still has one advantage chemical preparations don't—in addition to adding vital food elements to the soil, it improves the soil's structure by adding organic material. Well-rotted, commercially prepared manure can be bought by the bag at nurseries. Used according to the directions, it can do soil a world of good.

KNOW YOUR pH

Another soil factor is pH level, which determines how available various nutrients are to plants. You can have your soil's pH levels analyzed at a lab, but it's also possible to do this test yourself. Kits are available at most garden centers, and for the very dedicated there are sophisticated meters that work by inserting a sensor into the soil. In the 1930s, the authors of *America's Garden Book* considered pH testing something every home gardener should master, pointing out that rain, frequent watering, and fertilization all tended to make the soil grow more acidic over relatively short periods of time. The pHs in this book are based on the following scale:

pH Scale

pH Level	*Type of Soil*
9.5	Intensely alkaline
9.0	Strongly alkaline
8.5	Definitely alkaline
8.0	Moderately alkaline
7.5	Slightly alkaline
7.0	**Neutral**
6.5	Very slightly acid
6.0	Slightly acid
5.5	Moderately acid
5.0	Moderately acid
4.5	Definitely acid
4.0	Strongly acid
3.5	Intensely acid

—*America's Garden Book*, 1939

Nothing about the pH scale has changed over the years, nor has the fact that most plants prefer neutral soil—that is, soil that measures around 7.0 on the scale.

Like the Richter scale that measures earthquakes, each whole number on the pH scale is 10 times greater than the number before it. In other words, using 7.0 as a starting point, soil that measures 8.0 is ten times more alkaline than soil measuring 7.0, and 9.0 soil is 100 times more alkaline than neutral 7.0 soil. Soil that measures 6.0 is 10 times more acidic than 7.0 soil, and 5.0 soil is 10 times more acidic than that.

Each whole number indicates a ten-fold variation, so it's rare to find soils at either end of the scale. This is good as it's relatively easy to change soil by a half point or so, but nearly impossible to change it by several numbers.

- **IF SOIL IS TOO ACIDIC:** That's lucky. It's easier to raise soil pH than it is to lower it and an application of lime will work relatively quickly. Hydrated lime, ground limestone, and mixed lime are all available in commercial preparations at your garden store.

- **IF SOIL IS TOO ALKALINE:** Unfortunately, it's more difficult to lower the pH level than to raise it. One way is to add organic materials such as peat moss, compost, and well-rotted manure, as their decomposition will generate acids. However, since this chemical reaction is influenced by soil type, temperature, and other factors, results may be slow to come and difficult to calibrate. Soil can also be improved by adding sulfur or an acidifying fertilizer designed for high-alkaline soil types. As was previously noted, time is on your side—soil tends to become more acidic over the seasons.

TIPS FOR PREPARING AND CONDITIONING SOIL

Even the best soil will not produce well unless it's properly managed by remixing and enriching it. Here are some basic maintenance activities.

- **TURNING:** Before planting, soil should be prepared by digging it with a spade or garden fork. Dig one spit down—that is, the depth of the spade blade—and lift and turn the soil. Remove large stones, roots, and other debris. Then add fresh topsoil, humus, fertilizer, or other conditioners, working the new material thoroughly into the existing soil. If you are digging in the spring or summer, break up clumps and clods.

- **RIDGING:** Soil that is to lie fallow over the winter will benefit by ridging. To do this, leave clods unbroken and pile soil into ridges six to ten inches high. Winter freezing makes soil easier to break up in the spring, and kills many eggs left by insects.

- **DOUBLE DIGGING:** This requires a lot of effort, but it's an excellent, old-timer's way to prepare soil, especially for larger areas such as vegetable plots. To begin, dig a trench the length of the area that is one spit deep

SINGLE DIGGING
ONE SPIT DEEP

HOLD DIGGING FORK AS NEARLY UPRIGHT AS POSSIBLE AND DRIVE THE TINES INTO THE SOIL FULL DEPTH. MANY GARDENERS ARE CARELESS IN TURNING CLODS AND FAIL TO BREAK THEM WHILE SPADING—UNLESS THIS IS DONE IT WILL BE PRACTICALLY IMPOSSIBLE TO PULVERIZE THE SOIL LATER.

LEAVE CLODS UNBROKEN & ROUGH ONLY WHEN EXPOSED TO FREEZING

DOUBLE DIGGING
TWO SPITS DEEP

DOUBLE DIGGING

TOP SOIL

BOTTOM SOIL. SPADE IN CINDERS, SAND LEAVES, MANURE, ETC.

SOIL RIDGING IS USED IN WINTER TO EXPOSE A LARGER SURFACE FOR FREEZING

TRENCHING
THREE SPITS DEEP

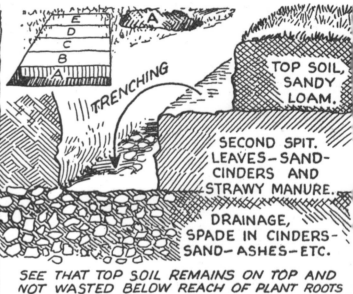

TRENCHING

TOP SOIL, SANDY LOAM.

SECOND SPIT. LEAVES—SAND—CINDERS AND STRAWY MANURE.

DRAINAGE, SPADE IN CINDERS—SAND—ASHES—ETC.

SEE THAT TOP SOIL REMAINS ON TOP AND NOT WASTED BELOW REACH OF PLANT ROOTS

and two feet wide. Completely remove the soil, dividing it in two piles, one at either end of the trench. To the bottom of the trench, add whatever conditioning materials are suited to your soil (compost, sand, humus, fertilizer, and so on). Now dig down another spit in depth, turning the soil and thoroughly mixing in the conditioning materials. When you have finished, dig an identical trench beside the first one, again completely removing the soil. Add conditioning materials to the new trench, and dig down another spit in depth, mixing and turning the soil. Now, fill the second trench with the earth you removed from the first trench, mixing in additional conditioning materials as you go. Repeat this process until you have worked your way across the entire plot, filling each trench with conditioning materials and the earth from the previous trench. Use the earth from the final trench to fill the first trench you dug. Properly done, double digging will last several years.

- **TRENCHING OR TRIPLE DIGGING:** This is similar to double digging, and only slightly more work. Begin with a trench that is one spit deep and two feet wide, as with double digging. Now, inside this first trench, dig another trench that is one spit deep and one spit wide, removing earth as you did before. Proceed as with double digging, adding conditioning materials and digging down another depth, and then filling the trench with soil from the previously dug trench mixed with additional conditioning material. As with double digging, triple digging need be undertaken just once every several seasons.

—adapted from *The Modern Family Garden Book*, 1941

It has been fittingly said that the lawn is the canvas upon which all architectural and landscape effects are produced. A rich carpet of grass is nature's outdoor Oriental, a source of beauty and pride that adds much to the enjoyment of the home and the things that the word home suggests.

—*Better Homes and Gardens*, June 1926

LUSH

Lawns

It's not clear when the first man-made lawns appeared, but they were certainly a part of the great royal gardens of Europe. In all probability, the lawn was a replication of the game preserve's sweeping meadow—tamed, reduced in size, and expertly landscaped to gracefully hug the palace or the manor house.

With the rise of the middle class during the industrial age, lawns became an emblem of home ownership, the proud establishment of each family's little domain. Patents for lawn mowers dating back to 1799 can be found in the British archives, and by the 1830s working models were being produced and sold. Britons, a nation of people curiously attached to their mowers, still venerate the machine, and have established a British Lawnmower Museum, open year round, in Southport, Lancashire, England. In addition to historic models from the past, the museum houses an especially sprightly collection entitled Lawnmowers of the Rich and Famous.

In America, where the lawn has come to represent suburbia in all its pains and glories, the relationship is more a love-hate affair. To look upon a velvet swath of deepest green is heartening. To wage eternal war against crabgrass, dandelion, and the neighbor's dog is not.

GRADING: THE BONES OF A GOOD LAWN

To a large extent, a lawn is only as good as what lies beneath it. This means not only soil that has been properly prepared, but soil that has been properly graded.

Grading (the shaping and contouring of the soil) accomplishes three things essential for a desirable lawn. First and foremost, it promotes proper drainage. Grass does not like waterlogged soil and will not flourish where surface water does not drain away. Second, a properly graded area is easier to care for and more conducive to growth. And, finally, good grading pleases the eye and enhances the house, trees, plantings, and other elements of the yard.

An ideally graded lawn slopes gradually, in a gen-

IDEAL GRADING.
LAWN SLOPES FROM HOUSE IN ALL DIRECTIONS

SIDE WALK

A SHALLOW GUTTER WILL KEEP SOIL FROM WASHING OVER SIDEWALK

DRAIN TILE   SIDE WALK

METHOD OF GRADING WHERE HOUSE IS LOWER THAN STREET.

WRONG

SIDE WALK

A STEEP FRONT LAWN APPEARS LARGER BY THIS METHOD

WRONG

A DIFFICULT JOB PROPERLY PLANTED AND GRADED

A STEEP BANK DWARFS THE APPARENT EXTENT OF THE LAWN

DRAIN TILE

WHERE THE LOT RISES IN THE REAR USE A WATER-BREAK FOR A DRY CELLAR

A PROPERLY GRADED LAWN LEADS THE EYE GENTLY UP-GRADE DECREASING THE APPARENT HEIGH

tly rolling curve, away from the house down to the street and property lines. Steep slopes are undesirable for a number of reasons. The steeper the slope, the more rapidly water runs off it, and the more likely topsoil is to erode. This makes grass difficult to grow. When grass does grow on a steep slope, it is difficult to mow and to maintain. Some lots feature steep gradations and gentle grading is impossible. If this is your problem, you may want to break the decline into a series of gentle terraces or use a retaining wall to create an "upper" and "lower" yard. If neither of these is feasible, consider using other types of ground cover (such as shrubs or ivies) that do well on steep inclines.

Lawns that contain dips and ditches cause a more difficult problem. If you can't build up these areas to improve drainage, you will either need to consider replacing grass with moisture-loving plants, or add a feature such as a small pool or water garden. If the ground is saturated, you may want to consider installing a drainage system.

NEW LAWN OR OLD?

There are only two reasons to make a new lawn: one is that you wish to have grass in places where it is not now growing and the other is that your current lawn is so bare and patchy, and the soil so hard-packed and inhospitable, that you have little choice but to start fresh. Unless this is the case, it is usually easier and less expensive to rehabilitate an existing lawn. However, creating a lawn from scratch is not a Herculean task. Since the first tract housing sprang up in the wake of World War II, millions of suburban pioneers have planted millions of acres of lawn.

The most common way to make a lawn today is with precut sod. In the past, this was considered the lazy way out, sure to produce unsatisfactory results. This isn't true—but it's important to know how to do it the old-fashioned way. Conditioning the soil is a must no matter which method you use, and every gardener should know how to grow grass from seed—it's an excellent way to reinvigorate worn spots and repair damaged patches.

From Seed to Lawn in Twenty Steps

1. Place stakes around the area to be reseeded.

2. With a spade, remove a strip of topsoil that runs the length of the area and measures four feet wide by four inches deep. Set it aside.

3. There is now an exposed section of subsoil that is ready to be conditioned.

   - IF SUBSOIL IS HARD CLAY: Spread with one inch of sand or two inches of fine ashes or cinders. If soil is overly acidic, add limestone to cover. Now add one to two inches of well-rotted manure, leaf mold, peat moss, or humus. (Some lawn clippings and leaves may be mixed in.)

   - IF SUBSOIL IS SANDY: Do not add sand or cinders but increase the amount of water-holding materials such as well-rotted manure, leaf mold, peat moss, or humus.

4. Work the added materials into the subsoil, making sure it is broken up finely.

5. Firm up the subsoil by tamping down.

6. Working alongside the area you have just prepared, remove a second strip of topsoil. Break up the soil and clean it of grass roots, large pebbles, and other debris.

7. Distribute this cleaned topsoil over the subsoil of the first strip that was dug.

Granted full Patent Protection by the U. S. Gov't because there is nothing else like it

RAIN KING

Adjustable to Volume, Distance and Direction—Whirling or Stationary

8. To the topsoil, add materials to make a desirable garden loam such as compost, humus, fine peat, leaf mold, and sand if the soil is clay-heavy or extra humus if the soil is sandy.

9. Work over the entire area in this way, always using the topsoil from the most recently dug strip to cover the subsoil of the strip dug before it.

10. When the whole area has been completed, work the topsoil again. If necessary, add more conditioning materials.

11. Water the area well, checking to see that it drains properly. If water is not absorbed into the soil and pools on top of it, drainage is poor and needs to be improved.

12. Wait several days before planting grass seed.

13. Roll the area twice, the second time at right angles to the first.

14. Sow the seed, using the amount recommended by the manufacturer. To avoid a stripe pattern and ensure even coverage, sow half the seeds crosswise and half lengthwise, and go over the area twice.

15. Rake the seed or cover with a little fine soil.

16. Roll with a light roller and sprinkle with water gently but well. Do not add chemical fertilizers until the grass is fully sprouted and then only in a very weak solution.

17. Keep seed moist until it has germinated (this will take a few days). Do this by tenting the area with muslin stretched over stakes or wire, and watering through the muslin.

18. When the seed has germinated, stake the muslin to a height of ten inches for a day or so to let the new grass harden.

19. Remove the muslin and allow full exposure to the sun.

20. Allow grass to grow to a height of three inches before cutting.

—adapted from *The Complete Book of Garden Magic*, 1935

TRANSFORMING A LACKLUSTER LAWN

If you have a lawn,
even a poor one,
it's probably easier
to restore its beauty
than to dig it up and
start over. Again, garden expert Roy Biles
offers sage advice in the pages of *The Complete
Book of Garden Magic*, 1935.

- First, examine your soil by digging down. It should
  have two to three inches of workable loam on top, and
  four to six inches of well-draining soil below.
- Prepare the lawn by removing weeds, fallen leaves, thatch,
  and other debris.
- Level or fill in low spots and depressions.
- Sow seeds across the entire area, using more
  in bare areas.
- Roll smooth.
- Apply chemical fertilizer to the entire
  lawn, making sure to wash well into the
  grass roots.
- If sowing in fall, apply one-half inch
  mulch composed of one part sand
  to two parts peat humus before
  fertilizing. The freezing and
  thawing of winter will work
  the mulch down into the grass
  roots and promote good spring
  growth. Doing this over a period of
  years will turn your
  lackluster lawn to
  rich green turf!

ROLL LAWN WHEN DAMP BUT NOT WET.

LEVEL UP DEPRESSIONS WITH GOOD SOIL

SEED BARE SPOTS WITH A GOOD MIXTURE OF GRASS SEED.

FERTILIZE GRASS WITH CHEMICA IF POSSIBLE, USE A SPREADER

TO ELIMINATE WIRE GRASS KEEP LAWN GRASS 3 IN. HIGH AFTER MAY 15th.

STAB SINGLE DANDELIONS WITH AN IRON ROD DIPPED IN ACID. *BRUISE AND SPRAY LARGE AREAS*

REMOVE PLANTIANS AND OTHER WEEDS WITH A WEED SPUD

WEAR RUBBER APRON AND GALOSHE

CHICKWEED, GROUND IVY AN ALL CREEPING WEEDS YIELD T A SPRAY OF SODIUM CHLORAT

KEEP OUT OF DOORS AND AWAY FROM FIRE

KILL ANTS BY SQUIRTING CARBON-BISULPHIDE* INTO THEIR RUNWAYS.

IN SUMMER, DRESS WITH COMPOST, MIXED WITH BONE MEAL.

10 FT
5 FT
2 FT
KEEP BOX COVERE

4" GOOD SOIL MIXED WITH 25% SAND
6 IN. PACKED WET LEAVES MIXE WITH CHEMICAL LAWN FOODS.

THE COMPOST BOX CAN HIDDEN WITH SHRUBBERY

* Carbon bisulphide is no longer commonly used. Consult your local gardening center for a substitute.

40

REPAIRING WORN PATCHES

Q.: Our lot is on a corner and there is a path worn across the lawn. The soil is hard there now. What can I do to get grass to grow?

A.: *The continuous packing down of turf results in squeezing fine soil particles together to the extent that air, food, and moisture cannot penetrate to the grass roots. To open up such soil a spike tamp may be used or even a fork resembling a pitchfork. Following this perforating, apply fertilizer and seed, then cover with straw, peat moss, or rotted manure.*

Of course, an area which is under such treatment ought to be fenced off if possible.

—*Flower Grower*, March 1944

STRAWBERRY LAWNS

Gardeners of the past were nothing if not creative. Here's a World War II solution to the I-hate-my-lawn problem that, sadly, never caught on.

The search for a distinctive ground cover goes on and on, and while Diachondra and ivy have proved adaptable for the purpose principally in the West and South, yet another unusual plant is being introduced as a front yard cover.

It's strawberries!

Cultivation of wild strawberry plants either along parkways or on broad expanses has definitely passed the experimental stage—and the results are good.

Such a lawn must not be ruled out in the city. Eight months after planting, under proper conditions, strawberry plants rival or exceed the heavy luster of ivy, now used extensively in place of grass in many metropolitan areas. Indeed, a carpet of strawberry plants offers less opportunity for weeds to grow than do most sensitive varieties of grass.

The ground should be deeply spaded and well mixed with humus—preferably leaf mold or peat moss—before planting, which is best done in the late fall or winter. Small plants may be set out about eighteen inches to two feet apart to establish a covering the following summer. Fall planting is not a requirement, however. In many cases the plants, placed one foot apart, have been started at odd seasons, producing a thick-matted cover in eight months.

With few exceptions a strawberry ground cover responds to virtually the same treatment as that given to grass lawns. Application of fertilizer—well-rotted barnyard manure or commercial brands—in the summer and the fall, with brief daily sprinkling, is necessary. Some gardeners have found that mowing of the plants three times a year, leaving a ruff two inches high, increases root development and thickens the growth.

Wild strawberries under suitable conditions offer a dense ground cover, enhancing the appearance of a yard with their dark, shiny leaves and, periodically, their small but colorful blossoms. Varieties produce blossoms of pink, red, white, or yellow and the plants bloom two or three times a year.

—adapted from *Flower Grower*, April 1943

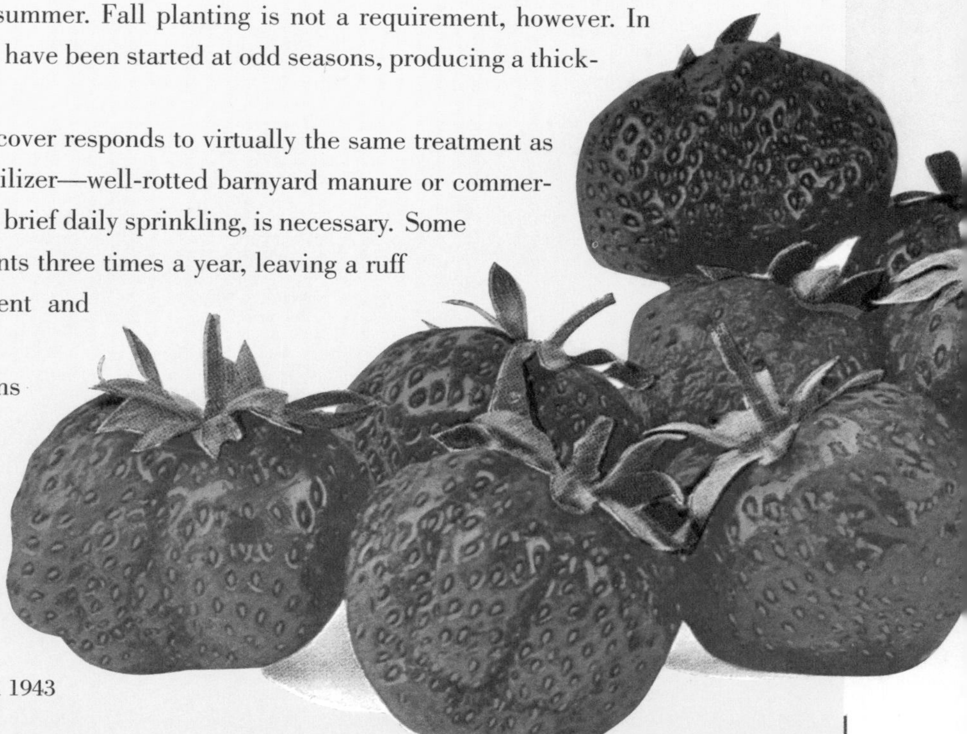

A Lawn of Velvety Green

WHAT LAWNS WANT

What does it take to maintain a lush green lawn? Here's a basic to-do list:

- **ROLLING:** This is necessary to do when winter freezing and heaving causes the roots to "lift" from the soil. Depending on the climate zone in which you live, rolling may or may not be appropriate. If it is, do it only once a year when the ground is moist but not wet enough to puddle when rolled. Rolling when the soil is dry is useless, and rolling when the ground is too wet will smother the roots.

- **WATERING:** Grass loves water, but how it is watered makes almost as much difference as how much water it gets. To be effective, water must penetrate the soil to a depth of four inches. This allows the grass to develop deep, strong roots— the kind of roots that sustain grass through hot, dry weather. Watering by hand is not effective because the water does not fall in any one spot long enough to soak into the ground. Inadequately watered grass has shallow roots and is more likely to die during periods of heat and drought. The best way to water a lawn is with a sprinkler or soaker hose. This allows each spot to receive a gentle, prolonged soaking. Water each spot for two to three hours at a time, at a rate that allows water to be continuously absorbed into the ground. How often you need to water depends on how much rainfall you receive. In general, a lawn built on clay soil requires at least one inch of water each week, and should receive water at least once a week. Sandy soil, which does not hold water as well, will need to be watered more than once a week.

- **MOWING:** In the quest to save time, it's tempting to give the lawn a buzz cut, one that will save us from repeating the task for a while! This, as every old-timer knows, is a mistake. Lawns that are cut too short in the hot summer months can become sunburned and dried out. For the best lawn, follow this routine:
    - **Spring through mid-May:** Cut grass to a height of 1½ inches. When grass is this short, and the weather is still relatively cool, clippings can be left on the ground to work back into the soil.
    - **Mid-May through September:** Maintain grass at a height of three inches. This will create shade and help keep the soil cool and moist. Clippings must be gathered and removed, as grass can be easily smothered in this weather.
    - **Final cut:** After the hot weather ends, you should give your lawn a good last mow, trimming it to about one inch before the winter.

- **WEEDING:** Weeds are opportunists, and the easiest way to foil them is to keep grass thick and healthy, depriving them of the space, air, and light they need to thrive. Since bare and worn spots are weed welcome mats, they should be reseeded or resodded as soon as possible. To discourage crabgrass, keep grass on the longish side—this creates a natural shade cover, and crabgrass will not germinate without plenty of sun. If weeds have gotten a toehold in your lawn, you will either need to dig them out by hand or use a commercial weed killer. In either case, make sure the entire root system is eliminated.

- **LAWN FERTILIZERS:** Achieving the deep, verdant green grass gardeners dream about requires a plentiful supply of nitrogen. Even if your lawn is rooted in good loam, you may want to use a topical (or top-dressing) fertilizer. If using a chemical fertilizer, choose one especially rich in nitrogen, such as ten parts nitrogen to four parts each phosphorus and potassium. Because chemical fertilizers are quickly washed away, you will need to re-fertilize every four to six weeks. Chemical fertilizers come in both dry and liquid forms. Whichever you use, water well after applying to wash the material into the roots.

Lawn maintenance is probably the single most time-consuming part of gardening—but the touch of cool, velvety grass between bare feet on a hot day makes it all worthwhile!

THE CRABGRASS PLAGUE

Q.: Every year our lawn is overrun with crabgrass. What can we do now to get rid of this pest?

A.: Crabgrass is an annual. If you keep it from going to seed and thus reinfesting your lawn you can, in time, get rid of it. Be sure that you cut it off and don't simply roll it down. The lawn should be raked up after one mowing and cut again crosswise. Be sure to remove and destroy the clippings. The time to be on the lookout for this common fall pest is in the late summer.

—*Flower Grower*, March 1944

The importance of trees to humans goes back to antiquity. Britons practiced forest management as far back as 4,700 years ago; 3,500 years ago, Egyptians imported trees from far-flung territories to be cultivated along the banks of the Nile. Druids assigned magical properties to trees, and both ancient and modern healers

Trees AND Shrubs

have formed medicines from bark and leaves. In America, the remnants of Johnny Appleseed's orchards still form a fragrant necklace across the heartland, and Arbor Day is still observed on the last Friday of April.

MAKING THE MOST OF TREES AND SHRUBS

When choosing trees or shrubs for your lawn or garden, you'll want to take several factors into consideration. A row of Lombardy poplars may look fine sweeping along the drive of a country estate in France, but altogether different edging a standard suburban lot. Elements to consider are:

- **GOALS:** Do you want a tree that provides shade or shrubs that create privacy or add interest to a particular area? Being clear about what you want will help you avoid expensive mistakes.

- **SUITABILITY:** Check with workers at a local nursery to make sure the type and variety of tree or shrub you've chosen is right for your climate, soil, and growing conditions.

- **SIZE:** It's easy to go "tree crazy" and create future problems by planting too many saplings—their root systems will soon take up a lot of soil space and your yard will eventually become too shady—just as it's easy to plant hedge shrubs so close together they soon compete with each other. Determine the eventual growth your trees and shrubs will achieve. Then, using one of the garden plans you made earlier, sketch in this information and plant accordingly.

- **SEASONS:** Consider how your selections will work with the rest of your plantings through each of the four seasons. For example, if your garden is already rich in spring blooms but a bit barren in the fall, you might choose a tree that gives brilliant autumn color over a dogwood that flowers in the spring.

- **COMPATIBILITY:** Consider how your tree will complement your house and neighborhood. Trees and shrubs should frame your house and give it presence, not make it stand out like a sore thumb.

ILL CHOSEN PLANTS SATISFY BUT A SHORT TIME

TOO MANY SIMILAR PLANTS KILL INTEREST

GET SLOPE FROM HOUSE AT CORNERS

THE BEST FOUNDATION PLAN AVOIDS MONOTONY BY TALL ACCENT PLANTS AND OFTEN EXPOSES PARTS OF FOUNDATION

EVERGREEN VINES WILL GROW UNDER EAVES AND IN PARTIAL SHADE.

DIG OUT ENTIRE AREA TO BE PLANTED—IT PAYS!

BEFORE PLANTING, ARRANGE BALLED PLANTS TO FIND BEST LOCATION.

2 IN. MULCH A MULCH IN JUNE IS LIKE AN UMBRELLA.

PROTECT FROM DOGS BY SPRAY OR FENCE.

GROWER'S GUIDE

SHADE TREES FOR STREETS

Deciduous: White Ash (*Fraxinus americana*), Western Catalpa (*Catalpa speciosa*), American Elm (*Ulmus americana*), Scotch Elm (*Ulmus glabra*), Ginkgo Biloba (*Salisburia adiantifolia*), American Sweet Gum (*Liquidambar styraciflua*), Hackberry (*Celtis* sp.), English Hawthorn (*Crataegus laevigata*), Japanese Tree Lilac (*Syringa reticulata*), Basswood or American Linden (*Tilia americana*), European Linden (*Tilia* x *europea*), Small-leaved European Linden (*Tilia cordata*), Magnolia (*Magnolia* sp.), Amur Maple (*Acer ginnala*), Norway Maple (*Acer platanoides*), Sugar Maple (*Acer saccharum*), Sycamore Maple (*Acer pseudoplatanus*), Tatarian Maple (*Acer tataricum*), Black Oak (*Quercus velutina*), Laurel Oak (*Quercus laurifolia*), Live Oak (*Quercus virginiana*), Mossy-Cup Oak (*Quercus macrocarpa*), Pin Oak (*Quercus palustris*), Red Oak (*Quercus rubra*), Scarlet Oak (*Quercus coccinea*), Spanish Oak (*Quercus falcata*), Willow Oak (*Quercus phellos*), Lombardy Poplar (*Populus nigra "Italica"*), White Poplar (*Populus alba*), London Plane Tree (*Platanus acerifolia*), Chinese Scholar Tree (*Sophora japonica*), Golden-Rain Tree (*Cassia fistula*), Cockspur Thorn (*Crataegus crusgalli*), Washington Thorn (*Crataegus phaenopyrum*)

TREES FOR DRY, SANDY SOIL

Deciduous: Wafer Ash (Hop Tree) (*Ptelea trifoliata*), Large-Toothed Aspen (*Populus grandidentata*), Quaking Aspen (*Populus tremuloides "aurea"*), European White Birch (*Betula pendula*), Gray Birch (*Betula populifolia*), Monarch Birch (*Betula maximowicziana*), Black Cherry (*Prunus serotina*), Sour Cherry (*Prunus cerasus*), Box Elder (*Acer negundo*), Black Locust (*Robinia pseudoacacia*), Amur Maple (*Acer ginnala*), Hedge Maple (*Acer campestre*), Tatarian Maple (*Acer tataricum*), Scarlet Oak (*Quercus coccinea*), Pignut (*Carya glabra*), White Poplar (*Populus alba*), Tree-of-Heaven (*Ailanthus altissima*)

Evergreen: Red Cedar (*Juniperus virginiana*), Pitch Pine (*Pinus rigida*), Scots Pine (*Pinus sylvestris*), Swiss Mountain Pine (*Pinus mugo*), White Pine (*Pinus strobus*), Canadian Spruce (*Picea glauca*), Norway Spruce (*Picea abies*)

TREES THAT THRIVE IN VERY WET SOIL

Deciduous: European Alder (*Alnus glutinosa*), Green Ash (*Fraxinus pennsylvanica*), Water Ash (*Fraxinus caroliniana*), Large-toothed Aspen (*Populus grandidentata*), Sweet Bay (*Laurus nobilis*), Gray Birch (*Betula populifolia*), River Birch (*Betula nigra*), Yellow Birch (*Betula lutea*), Buttonwood (*Conocarpus erectus*), Carolina Cottonwood (*Populus deltoides*), Bald Cypress (*Taxodium distichum*), Box Elder (*Acer negundo*), Sour Gum (*Nyssa sylvatica*), Tupelo (*Nyssa* sp.), American Sweet Gum (*Liquidambar styraciflua*), American Hornbeam (*Carpinus caroliniana*), Shagbark Hickory (*Carya ovata*), American Linden (*Tilia americana*), Water Locust (*Gleditsia aquatica*), Red Maple (*Acer rubrum*), Silver Maple (*Acer saccharinum*), Pin Oak (*Quercus palustris*), Swamp white Oak (*Quercus bicolor*), Willow Oak (*Quercus phellos*), Black Willow (*Salix nigra*), Brittle Willow (*Salix fragilis*), Golden Willow (*Salix alba "vitellina"*), Laurel Willow (*Salix pentandra*), Weeping Willow (*Salix babylonica*), White Willow (*Salix alba*)

Evergreen: American Arborvitae (*Thuja occidentalis*), White Cedar (*Chamaecyparis thyoides*), Balsam Fir (*Abies balsamea*), Hemlock (*Conium maculatum*), Black Spruce (*Picea mariana*), Red Spruce (*Picea rubens*)

TREES THAT GROW RAPIDLY

Deciduous: European Mountain Ash (*Sorbus aucuparia*), White Ash (*Fraxinus americana*), Black Cherry (*Prunus serotina*), Cucumber Tree (*Magnolia acuminata*), American Elm (*Ulmus americana*), Scotch Elm (*Ulmus glabra*), Empress Tree (*Paulownia tomentosa*), Gray Birch (*Betula populifolia*), Monarch Birch (*Betula maximowicziana*), Western Catalpa (*Catalpa speciosa*), Box Elder (*Acer negundo*), Ginkgo Biloba (*Salisburia adiantifolia*), European Larch (*Larix decidua*), Japanese Tree Lilac (*Syringa reticulata*), American Linden (*Tilia americana*), Black Locust (*Robinia pseudoacacia*), Honey Locust (*Gleditsia triacanthos*), Umbrella Magnolia (*Magnolia tripetala*), Norway Maple (*Acer platanoides*), Red Maple (*Acer rubrum*), Silver Maple (*Acer saccharinum*), Pin Oak (*Quercus palustris*), London Plane Tree (*Platanus acerifolia*), Lombardy Poplar (*Populus nigra "Italica"*), White Poplar (*Populus alba*), Tree-of-Heaven (*Ailanthus altissima*), Tulip Tree (*Liriodendron tulipfera*), Golden Willow (*Salix alba "vitellina"*), White Willow (*Salix alba*)

Evergreen: Pitch Pine (*Pinus rigida*), Red Pine (*Pinus resinosa*), Scots Pine (*Pinus sylvestris*), White Pine (*Pinus strobus*), Norway Spruce (*Picea abies*)

TREES FOR THE SEASHORE

Deciduous: Quaking Aspen (*Populus tremuloides "aurea"*), Paper Birch (*Betula papyrifera*), Black Cherry (*Prunus serotina*), Carolina Cottonwood (*Populus deltoides*), English Hawthorn (*Crataegus laevigata*), American Hornbeam (*Carpinus caroliniana*), European Hornbeam (*Carpinus betulus*), Honey Locust (*Gleditsia triacanthos*),

Red Maple (*Acer rubrum*), Sycamore Maple (*Acer pseudoplatanus*), Laurel Oak (*Quercus laurifolia*), Live Oak (*Quercus virginiana*), Red Oak (*Quercus rubra*), American Plane Tree (*Platanus occidentalis*), Beach Plum (*Prunus maritima*), White Poplar (*Populus alba*), Sassafras (*Sassafras albidum*), White Willow (*Salix alba*)

Evergreen: Red Cedar (*Juniperus virginiana*), Creeping Juniper (*Juniperus horizontalis*), Austrian Pine (*Pinus nigra*), Cluster Pine (*Pinus pinaster*), Japanese Black Pine (*Pinus thunbergiana*), Pitch Pine (*Pinus rigida*), Swiss Mountain Pine (*Pinus mugo*)

TREES THAT FORM GOOD WINDBREAKS

Deciduous: Amur Maple (*Acer ginnala*), Box Elder (*Acer negundo*), Downy Hawthorn (*Crataegus mollis*), White Mulberry (*Morus alba*), Pin Oak (*Quercus palustris*), Osage Orange (*Maclura pomifera*), Balsam Poplar (*Populus bal-samifera*), White Poplar (*Populus alba*), Laurel Willow (*Salix pentandra*), White Willow (*Salix alba*)

Evergreen: American Arborvitae (*Thuja occidentalis*), Red Cedar (*Juniperus virginiana*), Hemlock (*Conium macula-tum*), Austrian Pine (*Pinus nigra*), Japanese Black Pine (*Pinus thunbergiana*), Pitch Pine (*Pinus rigida*), Scots Pine (*Pinus sylvestris*), White Pine (*Pinus strobus*), Western Yellow Pine (*Pinus ponderosa*), Canadian Spruce (*Picea glauca*), Norway Spruce (*Picea abies*), Red Spruce (*Picea rubens*)

SHRUBS FOR SPECIAL PURPOSES

LOW HEDGES, SHEARED OR UNSHEARED: Japanese Barberry (*Berberis thunbergii*), Regal Privet (*Ligustrum obtusifolium "Regelianum"*)

TALL HEDGES, UNSHEARED: Althaea (*Hibiscus syriacus*), Ibota Privet (*Ligustrum ibota*), Ibolium Privet (*Ligustrum* x *ibolium*)

TALL HEDGES, SHEARED: Amur Maple (*Acer ginnala*), Amur Privet (*Ligustrum amurense*)

BACKGROUND SHRUBS FOR FLOWER BORDERS: Althaea (*Hibiscus syriacus*), Ibota Privet (*Ligustrum ibota*), Virginal Mock Orange (*Philadelphus virginalis*)

LOW SHRUBS FOR SHADY LOCATIONS: Alpine Currant (*Ribes alpinum*), Coralberry (*Aechmea fulgens*), Fragrant Sumac (*Rhus aromatica*), Regal Privet (*Ligustrum obtusifolium "Regelianum"*)

FLOWERING SHRUBS FOR SUNNY LOCATIONS: Buddleia (*Buddleia davidii*), Deutzia (*Deutzia* sp.), Lilac (*Syringa vulgaris*), Spirea (*Spirea* sp.), Weigela (*Weigela* sp.)

HOW TO PLANT TREES AND SHRUBS

Unless you want to plant directly from an acorn and have a good half-century to spare, you will be transplanting rather than planting trees. For this reason, it is best to get your plants from a reputable nursery, one that will provide you with a healthy, thriving plant that has been properly nurtured and prepared. Trees and shrubs from the wild may be inexpensive, but their root sys-

tems have often grown so wide they cannot be safely dug up. If you wish to transplant a specimen from the wild, or an established tree from another part of your yard, you will need to prune the roots a year in advance to encourage the formation of a manageable root ball (see "Root Pruning," page 58.) Trees are expensive, long-term investments, and it is always worthwhile to buy the best specimens you can afford. If you have purchased a very large tree, you may want to have it professionally planted, but smaller trees and shrubs can easily be transplanted by amateur gardeners.

In transplanting as in comedy, timing is essential. Most shrubs can be safely planted in all seasons but winter, provided they have been pruned and prepared with this in mind. For most deciduous trees and shrubs, the best time to transplant is in the fall (after the onset of the tree's dormant period) and early spring (until the time sap begins to run and budding and leafing begin). However, if you live in an area with long, severe winters, early spring—after the soil has warmed and is dry enough to work with—is preferable. Spring planting is also considered essential for the magnolia, flowering dogwood, birch, sweet gum, tupelo, black walnut, bald cypress, poplar, and tulip tree.

If you have a choice of days, a still, moist, overcast day is best—when transplanting trees and shrubs, it's important for the plants' roots to retain moisture. If you must work on a dry, sunny, windy day, wait until the cool of late afternoon or evening.

Once you have the tree or shrub selected, planting is relatively simple. Just follow these steps:

1. Dig a hole that is two feet deep and at least one foot wider than the reach of the roots in every direction.

2. Break up the soil at the bottom of the hole with a spade. If soil is hard and clay-heavy, work in some sand, cinders, or ash. Water-retaining materials such as peat or leaf mold should also be worked in. The soil excavated from the hole can be prepared in the same manner. (At this stage, well-rotted manure should not be used as it may burn roots.) For shrubs and hedges, best results are gained by trenching or triple digging, as described on page 33. Since hedges are planted close together, it's important that the soil be well prepared.

3. Fill the hole with the amount of conditioned, excavated soil that will allow you to plant the tree at the same depth it has been growing at. (Gauge this by checking the dirt ring around the trunk.)

4. Now flood the hole with water. This allows the bottom soil to settle and gives you an opportunity to check and correct the drainage.

5. After the water has drained completely, place the shrub or tree in the hole, laying the roots out naturally. Using your hands and feet, work the soil under and around the roots to make sure there are no air pockets. If you use a shovel or spade, make sure you don't inadvertently nick the roots.

6. When the hole is about two-thirds full, you can use your feet to pack down the soil firmly.

7. Flood the hole with water one more time to compact the soil and destroy any air pockets.

8. Loosely add the remaining soil. Do not tamp it down but *do* grade it so that water will drain toward the trunk—a crater shape rather than a mountain shape.

9. If the tree is good-sized, you will want to brace it with wires. (See "How to Straighten a Tree," page 58.)

RAPID RECOVERY SECRET

To keep the soil about newly planted trees in condition and to eliminate the competition of grass roots, the soil may be cultivated, and a mulch of well-rotted manure, straw, leaves, or peat moss may be spread to a depth of two to three inches over the area occupied by the roots.

After spring planting, the mulch may remain on the ground for two to three months and then should be worked into the ground by shallow spading, taking care not to reach the tree roots. After autumn planting, the mulch should remain on the surface all winter to minimize the effect of alternate freezing and thawing, and should be worked into the soil in the spring. A lasting benefit to the trees will result from applying a mulch each autumn for several years after transplanting. Then when the trees are well started, and the ground is in good condition, these circles under the trees may be sown to grass.

—America's Garden Book, 1939

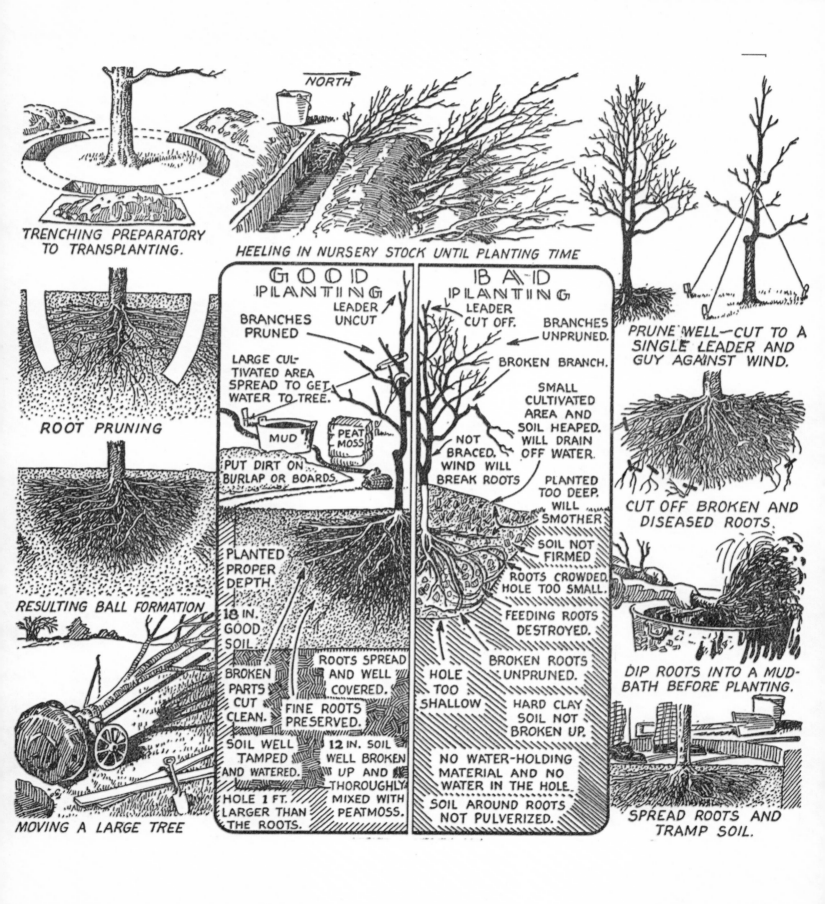

TRENCHING PREPARATORY TO TRANSPLANTING.

NORTH

HEELING IN NURSERY STOCK UNTIL PLANTING TIME

PRUNE WELL—CUT TO A SINGLE LEADER AND GUY AGAINST WIND.

ROOT PRUNING

RESULTING BALL FORMATION

MOVING A LARGE TREE

GOOD PLANTING

LEADER UNCUT

BRANCHES PRUNED

LARGE CULTIVATED AREA SPREAD TO GET WATER TO TREE.

MUD PEAT MOSS

PUT DIRT ON BURLAP OR BOARDS.

PLANTED PROPER DEPTH.

18 IN. GOOD SOIL

BROKEN PARTS CUT CLEAN.

ROOTS SPREAD AND WELL COVERED.

FINE ROOTS PRESERVED.

SOIL WELL TAMPED AND WATERED.

12 IN. SOIL WELL BROKEN UP AND THOROUGHLY MIXED WITH PEATMOSS.

HOLE 1 FT. LARGER THAN THE ROOTS.

BAD PLANTING

LEADER CUT OFF.

BRANCHES UNPRUNED.

BROKEN BRANCH.

SMALL CULTIVATED AREA AND SOIL HEAPED. WILL DRAIN OFF WATER.

NOT BRACED. WIND WILL BREAK ROOTS

PLANTED TOO DEEP. WILL SMOTHER

SOIL NOT FIRMED

ROOTS CROWDED, HOLE TOO SMALL.

FEEDING ROOTS DESTROYED.

HOLE TOO SHALLOW

BROKEN ROOTS UNPRUNED.

HARD CLAY SOIL NOT BROKEN UP.

NO WATER-HOLDING MATERIAL AND NO WATER IN THE HOLE.

SOIL AROUND ROOTS NOT PULVERIZED.

CUT OFF BROKEN AND DISEASED ROOTS.

DIP ROOTS INTO A MUD-BATH BEFORE PLANTING.

SPREAD ROOTS AND TRAMP SOIL.

SUMMER PLANTING

Although summer planting isn't ideal, it's sometimes unavoidable. That was the case during the busy, short-handed years of World War II when P. J. Van Mele, professional gardener, offered these tips for success:

- Choose plants which are the most likely to survive spring and fall transplantings, such as those with dense root systems. Avoid plants with tap roots and weak or damaged roots.
- Only work with trees and shrubs whose roots are surrounded by substantial earth balls which can be moved without breaking.
- Do not transplant during periods of "soft" growth (flowering and budding of leaves, for example.)
- Evergreens which grow continuously (such as junipers and arborvitaes) can be moved in both early and mid-summer. Evergreens which make only one annual shoot (such as pines, spruces, and firs) should not be moved until this shoot is fully matured, after mid-summer.
- If the ground is dry, soak it with water prior to digging, then prepare it as for spring and fall planting.
- If the root ball has become dry, water it well, make sure it is wrapped in damp cloth, and leave it in a closed garage or shed overnight.
- Avoid shocking the plants with ice cold water and do not over-water.
- Do not prune trees or shrubs that have been transplanted in the summer until the next season.

—*The Home Garden*, August 1944

WATERING EVERGREENS

Fall watering is especially important for evergreens. The ground should be soaked to below the frost line before it freezes over each fall, using a hose without a nozzle and with a gentle stream of water. This enables the roots to supply moisture to replace that which the winter sun draws from the foliage and a tree will be much more likely to come through severe weather without weakening.

—*The Complete Book of Garden Magic*, 1935

TREES AND WATER

Trees contain an amazing amount of water—as much as forty gallons in a medium-sized tree—and as much as twenty-five percent of this can evaporate on a hot, dry day. Water is an essential nutrient for a tree of any age and is especially crucial for newly planted trees. Thinking about how tree roots grow—both wide and deep—helps to understand how to go about watering them. To provide water to outlying roots, the entire area beneath the leaves should be well-watered. In the case of tall, narrow trees such as evergreens and certain shrubs, it's important to water well beyond the reach of the foliage. Frequent, light watering is not beneficial because the moisture won't penetrate deep-growing roots. It's better to water less frequently and to provide a long, slow drink which will penetrate deep into the ground. In warm, dry weather, water established trees once every ten days and newly planted trees once a week. Proper grading, as mentioned on page 54, also helps channel water to the tree roots.

In addition to supplying nutrients, water serves another purpose. Old-timers know that rain helps trees fight disease and infestation by keeping foliage clean. This is especially important for evergreens, which don't have a chance to shed old foliage. During dry spells, make sure trees and shrubs get a good bath occasionally.

ARE YOUR TREES WELL FED?

Whether or not you need to fertilize your trees will depend on the soil they grow in. Over-fertilization can injure the tree and lay down a welcome mat for borers and other parasites. Unless a tree shows signs of poor nourishment, think twice before you fertilize. Here's how to identify common nutrient deficiencies:

Symptom: Dwarfish plants, yellowish color.
Cause: Lack of nitrogen

Symptom: Dwarfish plants, grayish color.
Cause: Lack of phosphorus or potash.

Symptom: Yellowed leaf, uniform all over leaf.
Cause: Lack of iron or excess of lime, potash, magnesium, manganese, sodium, or carbonates.

Symptom: Yellowed leaf, patchy, spreading from midrib outward.
Cause: Lack of magnesium.

Symptom: Yellowed leaf, mottled.
Cause: Lack of lime.

Symptom: Yellowed leaf, spotty.
Cause: Lack of potash.

Symptom: Yellowed leaf, drying from tip and edges inward.
Cause: Lack of potash.

Symptom: Yellowed leaf, drying from midrib outward.
Cause: Lack of nitrogen.

Symptom: Brown patches on leaf, resembling scorch marks.
Cause: Lack of potash.

Symptom: Brown patches on leaf chiefly in center.
Cause: Lack of magnesium.

Symptom: Dark leaves with tendency to crinkle.
Cause: Too little potash in relationship to amount of nitrogen.

HOW TO PRUNE TREES AND SHRUBS

No greater crimes are committed against our plants than in the name of pruning. Often the ignorant workman or the gardener becomes too enthusiastic. The use of the small knowledge necessary will save much grief.

—*The Complete Book of Garden Magic*, 1935

Knowing how and when to prune is a must for every gardener—largely so doing it the wrong way and at the wrong time can be avoided. Because a tree grows best when the circumference of its crown is equal to the circumference of its roots, trees that have been root pruned will also need to have their crowns pruned. Other reasons for pruning are to improve the symmetry of the plant, to guide its growth, to rejuvenate an older plant, to remove dead or injured limbs, and to increase blossom or fruit production. Trees that have been purchased from a nursery, and arrive with a substantial root ball, should not be pruned.

THE THREE GOLDEN RULES OF PRUNING

- **PRUNE AT THE PROPER TIME:** For most deciduous trees, this is winter or early spring, although not for elms and maples which should be pruned in the late summer or fall to avoid "bleeding" of saps and fluids. Shrubs do best when pruned in the spring and summer, but flowering trees and shrubs should not be pruned until their blossoms have flowered and fallen. Spring is the best time for evergreens, though what month depends on where you live. Evergreens grow by producing one central shoot each year, and it's important to let this shoot mature before pruning is done.

- **PAY ATTENTION TO TOOLS:** Make sure shears are strong and sharp. Dull shears will cause bruising and tearing and may injure the entire plant. Use a pruning saw to remove large limbs.

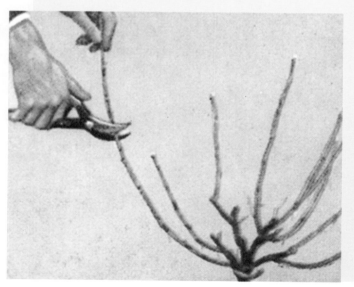

- **CUT UP:** Hold shears so the cut is made upward—not downward, horizontally, or diagonally. This reduces the chance of damaging the bark.

TRIMMING BRANCHES

This is by far the most common kind of pruning, and one that's well worth your while to master. First, decide how far back you want to cut the branch and look for a vigorous bud in this area; you will make your cut just beyond this bud. Determining which bud to cut near, and at what angle to cut, allows you to influence the plant's shape. For example, most trees and shrubs have "inside" and "outside" buds; inside buds point towards the center of the plant and outside buds point away from it. When the cut is made just beyond an outside bud, the growth will be outward, creating an open, spreading shape. If you prefer a shape that is more compact and vertical, you might want to cut at an inside bud. Once you've decided where to prune, make the cut on a slight diagonal, with the bud at the top, as shown in the illustration below.

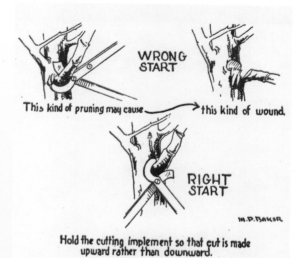

WRONG START

This kind of pruning may cause → this kind of wound.

RIGHT START

m.P.Baker

Hold the cutting implement so that cut is made upward rather than downward.

CUTTING AN ENTIRE BRANCH OR LIMB

For the health of the plant, branches that are dead or diseased must be completely removed from the tree as soon as possible. As the illustration at the right shows, the branch should be removed with a perpendicular cut as close to the trunk as possible, with no stump or protrusion left behind. If the branch is on a shrub, this can be done with a single cut of your shears. If the branch is a large or heavy limb, however, you should use a saw and remove the limb in stages. First, cut off most of the limb to remove the weight. Then, make a cut upward from the bottom at the point where the branch joins the tree trunk. Finish by cutting down from the top, until the cuts meet and the stump of the branch falls off. If the branch is sizable and the wound is large, it should be sealed with liquid asphalt or commercial tree dressing to prevent decay and promote the formation of a callus.

PRUNING HEDGES

Young plants should be pruned until they acquire the thick, dense foliage desirable in hedges. After that, they should be trimmed to prevent them from becoming too tall and to maintain a neat appearance. Some people are intimidated by the prospect of cosmetic shearing, convinced they will create the equivalent of a lopsided haircut. This needn't be the case, and trimming a hedge can be simple. The easiest way to ensure an even hedge is the method recommended by the authors of *The Popular Mechanics Garden Book*, in 1943. First, drive posts into the ground at intervals along the hedge. How many posts you will need depends on the length of your hedge. In general, place them at intervals of ten feet or so. The posts need not be driven deeply (they are only temporary), but they should be firm and upright. Now measure from the ground up to the height you want your hedge to be and make a mark on each post. Run wire, twine, or string from mark to mark along the posts, making sure there is no sag. Now all you have to do is trim the hedge to the level of your guide wires. This simple method spares the error that comes with "eyeballing" and it ensures that the hedge will be uniform even if it is on a slope.

THE PERFECT CUT

WRONG CUTS STEM WILL DIE BACK ALWAYS CUT TO A BUD THAT POINTS IN THE DIRECTION IN WHICH THE PLANT SHOULD GROW

PRUNING AN EVERGREEN HEDGE

Q.: *I have a hemlock hedge that I would like to keep 5 ft. high. When should it be pruned?–R.I.*

A.: *Best time to clip an evergreen hedge is in late June (in the North). One clipping a year is usually sufficient. Clip your hedge to about 5 ft. high in very early spring next year, and then annually after that in late summer.*

—The Home Garden, February 1944

PRUNING A GAP IN A HEDGE

When a gap is found in the hedge, the bush at one side is trimmed of all its branches, and cut partially through, close to the ground with an upward cut, on the side away from the gap. This cut should be sufficiently deep to allow the stem to be bent to the ground without breaking off. If the laid stem reaches across the gap and beyond the next strong bush, it may be pegged down with a strong hooked peg or two. A healthy stem will sprout along its whole length the following season, and the gap is soon fully furnished. The stem should be cut close to the ground, so that when laid over it may lie on the ground. If the bark is notched at the places where it touches the ground it will send out roots at those parts, and so support the new growth. If it does not lie on the ground, this cannot occur, and also small dogs, pigs, etc. may be able to creep under it. Where the gap is too wide for this, a corresponding stem may be trimmed and cut at the other side of the gap, and laid in the opposite direction. If the two laid stems overlap, so much the better.

—House & Garden, April 1912

ROOT PRUNING

ROOT PRUNING CORDON FRUIT TREES

As noted earlier in this chapter, trees and shrubs that are being transplanted should be root pruned several months before being moved. For a tree, dig a trench around it. The larger the tree, the larger your trench should be in depth and circumference. When you have completed the trench, fill it with compost (not manure) or earth rich in moisture-holding material. The practice of trenching in this way will encourage the formation of a dense, fibrous root ball. If you are transplanting a small shrub, you can accomplish this without digging a trench. Simply spade a circumference around the plant, then fertilize close to the plant. For best results, root prune at least six months before you intend to move the plant.

HOW TO STRAIGHTEN A TREE

Often, through incorrect planting, uneven lighting, or the whims of growth, a tree will become crooked and need to be straightened. The younger the plant, the easier this task will be, but even older trees can, with time and patience, be returned to an upright position. The most important thing to remember when straightening a tree is to protect the bark from injury—always pad straightening ropes and cables with several thicknesses of cloth or similar material. Old beach towels and sections of tire work very well, and a good old-timer's trick is to thread the cable through a length of thick garden hose.

A PIECE OF SHEET METAL 12 IN. WIDE WILL KEEP CATS OUT OF TREES

To straighten a tree, thoroughly soak the ground around the base of the tree to loosen the soil. Using a block and tackle, and length of rope or cable, make a loose loop around the tree in the direction the tree needs to move. Run the rope to a notched post set firmly into the ground several feet from the tree. The post should be the same height as the loop around the tree, so that the cable is roughly horizontal. Tighten the rope a bit over a period of weeks until the tree is perpendicular. Once the tree is upright, the tree should be braced with a post and wires until its new position is firmly established.

THE CAT-TREE PROBLEM SOLVED!

Cats should be kept out of trees. This can easily be done by fastening a strip of sheet metal 18 inches long loosely about the tree four or five feet from the ground; it will prevent the use of its upper branches by any kinds of animals except birds. The cat climbs the tree by sinking its claws into the bark. It cannot sink its claws into the sheet metal. The metal can be painted to make it inconspicuous.

—*The Complete Book of Garden Magic*, 1935

A WORD ABOUT MAINTENANCE AND REPAIR

The best way to keep any tree or shrub healthy is to remember that bark serves the same purpose as skin does for animals—that is, it prevents infection and disease from getting from the outside to the inside. People may think that pests and insects "bore their way" into trees, but many are merely opportunists that take advantage of openings made by even slight injuries. Therefore, inspect your trees regularly for signs of damage to the bark, and attend to each problem as it arises. Dead, injured, or diseased material should be removed at once to prevent rot and decay. Small wounds can be disinfected and treated with a sealant. Large holes inside the trunk should be scraped clean and, if you value the tree, are best left to the services of a professional.

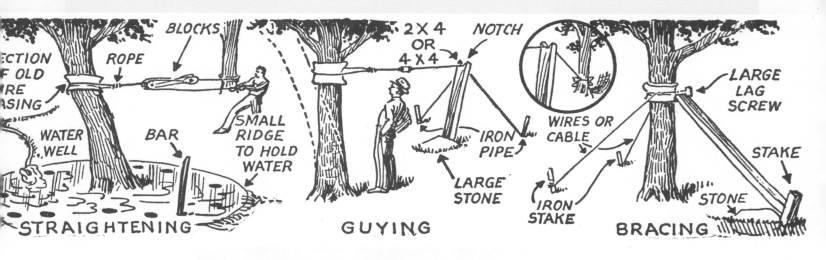

STRAIGHTENING — SECTION OF OLD WIRE CASING, WATER WELL, BAR, BLOCKS, ROPE, SMALL RIDGE TO HOLD WATER

GUYING — 2X4 OR 4X4, NOTCH, IRON PIPE, LARGE STONE, IRON STAKE, WIRES OR CABLE

BRACING — LARGE LAG SCREW, STAKE, STONE

If you've ever bought an irresistibly beautiful plant that looked all wrong once it was planted, you aren't alone. The biggest mistake made by gardeners is succumbing to this kind of temptation, ending up with a hodgepodge of plants that, while individually

PLANNING A FLOWER

Garden

lovely, do not harmonize or thrive in the space allotted them.

Since flowers are the single most important part of most gardens, it's worth time and planning to make sure they're shown to their best advantage.

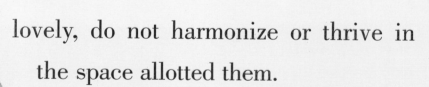

To do this, refer to the general garden plan made earlier and draw an accurately proportioned outline for each of your flower beds. Make the sketches large so that a detailed plan within each flower bed can be created.

When we think of a garden, our visual image is fairly certain to center around the English flower border, laid out in great drifts of glowing color, relieved by masses of white lilies and accented with towering spires of blue. . . . It is good to keep this picture in our minds. It expresses the beauty of form and color that every real lover of flowers tries to create to the best of his ability and resources. He may have only a dozen plants, but if they are well-grown and cared for, he has created a measure of beauty.

—The Complete Book of Garden Magic, 1935

The first thing to consider is what type of flower bed you have. One hundred years ago, when collars were starched and lawns were large and sweeping, it was fashionable to scatter circular, diamond, or star-shaped flower beds across the lawn. If you have the space and want to cultivate a Victorian look, you might experiment with one of these. The plan for such a bed should place the tallest plants at the center, then work outward with plants of descending height. More often, flowers are planted in border beds abutting a house, fence, walkway, and property line. These beds should be planned with the tallest plants at the back of the bed (farthest from the viewer's eye), and the shortest plants closest to the front. Here are some other things to keep in mind when planning flower beds:

- Avoid an arrangement that is too regular and predictable. While the tallest plants should generally be kept to the rear, a few of these should come forward to break up the height lines and add the charm of irregularity.

- Keep height in proportion to the bed. If a bed is very narrow, tall plants should be avoided except as accent notes.
- Plant varieties in clumps that are wider than they are deep rather than in single neat rows.
- Make sure each species planted has a strong but not overwhelming presence. It should be instantly identifiable and noticeable. However, too much of one species makes for a boring, static bed and if the species fails, spoils the flower bed for the season.

- Plan for continuous bloom. With a little fore-thought, you can enjoy a show of color from spring until autumn, and a bed that changes from week to week is far more interesting to look at as well as to tend.
- Work with a color scheme in mind. What colors you choose are up to you, but remember that strong, bright colors like red can overwhelm more delicate pastels and should be separated by greenery or neutral blooms in white or cream.
- Choose species that are suited for your conditions. Ultimately, you will be happier with a plant that thrives, even if it is your second choice, than with a "dream flower" that withers and dies.

—adapted from Home Flower Growing, 1928

FLOWERS FOR SPECIAL CONDITIONS

FLOWERS THAT GROW IN LIGHT SHADE

Annuals: Basket Flower (*Centaurea americana*), Chinese Forget-Me-Not (*Cynoglossum amabile*), Clarkia (*Clarkia rubicunda*), Drummond Phlox (*Phlox drummondii*), Lupine (*Lupinus* sp.), Pansy (*Viola* sp.), Snapdragon (*Antirrhinum* sp.), Sweet Alyssum (*Lobularia maritima*), Sweet-Sultan (*Centaurea moschata*)

Perennials: Bee Balm (*Monarda didyma*), Bethlehem Lungwort (*Pulmonaria saccharata*), Blackberry Lily (*Belmacanda chinensis*), Columbine (*Aquilegia* sp.), Common Foxglove (*Digitalis purpurea*), Coral Bells (*Heuchera sanguinea*), Cow Parsnip (*Heracleum lanatum*), Cowslip Primrose (*Primula veris*), Globeflower (*Trollius europaeus*), Hare Bell (*Campanula rotundifolia*), Japanese Anemone (*Anemone hupehensis*), Leopard's-Bane (*Doronicum caucasicum*), Peat Pink (*Dianthus* sp.), Pink Turtlehead (*Chelone lyonii*), Woodruff (*Asperula* sp.)

FLOWERS THAT GROW IN HEAVIER SHADE

Annuals: Calliopsis (*Calliopsis tinctoria*), Cockscomb (*Celosia cristata*), Godetia (*Clarkia amoena*), Impatiens or Garden Balsam (*Impatiens balsamina*), Lobelia (*Lobelia* sp.), Monkey Flower (*Mimulus* sp.)

Perennials: Azure Monkshood (*Aconitum carmichaelii*), Big Plantain Lily (*Hosta* sp.), Blue Plantain Lily (*Hosta* sp.), Bunchberry (*Cornus canadensis*), Cardinal Flower (*Lobelia cardinalis*), Christmas Rose (*Helleborus niger*), Dwarf Perpetual Forget-Me-Not (*Myosotis scorpioides semperflorens*), Fringed Bleeding-Heart (*Dicentra eximia*), Geneva Bugle (*Ajuga genevensis*), Lily-of-the-Valley (*Convallaria majalis*), Low Meadow Rue (*Thalictrum minus*), Rue Anemone (*Anemonella thalictroides*), Shooting Star (*Dodecatheon* sp.), Small Solomon's seal (*Polygonatum biflorum*), Snow Trillium (*Trillium nivale*), Virginia Bluebells (*Mertensia virginica*), Willow Amsonia (*Amsonia tabernaemontana*)

FLOWERS THAT GROW IN WET SOIL

Perennials: Bee Balm (*Monarda didyma*), Blue Flag (*Iris versicolor*), Cardinal Flower (*Lobelia cardinalis*), Cinnamon Fern (*Osmunda cinnamomea*), Eulalia (*Miscanthus sinensis*), Forget-Me-Not (*Myosotis* sp.), Loosestrife (*Lysimachia* sp.), Marsh Marigold (*Caltha palustris*), Pitcher Plant (*Darlingtonia purpurea*), Rose Mallow (*Hibiscus* sp.), Royal Fern (*Osmunda regalis*), Sensitive Fern (*Onoclea sensibilis*), Siberian Iris (*Iris sibirica*), Yellow Flag (*Iris pseudacorus*)

FLOWERS THAT GROW IN DRY, SANDY SOIL

Perennials: Bigleaf Statice (*Limonium* sp.), Flowering Spurge (*Euphorbia corollata*), Geneva Bugle (*Ajuga genevensis*), Golden Glow (*Rudbeckia laciniata*), Grass Pink (*Dianthus plumarius*), Iceland Poppy (*Papaver nudicaule*), Maltese Cross (*Lychnis chalcedonica*), New England Aster (*Aster novae-angliae*), Poppy Mallow (*Callirhoe involucrata*), Sunflower (*Helianthus annuus*), Wild Senna (*Cassia hebecarpa*), Yellow Camomile (*Anthemis tinctoria*), Yucca (*Yucca glauca*)

FLOWERS THAT WILL GROW IN VERY POOR SOIL

Annuals: California Poppy (*Eschscholzia californica*), Calliopsis (*Calliopsis tinctoria*), Corn Poppy (*Papaver rhoeas*), Feather Cockscomb (*Celosia cristata plumosa*), Four-O'clock (*Mirabilis jalapa*), Gaillardia (*Gaillardia* sp.), Impatiens or Garden Balsam (*Impatiens balsamina*), Love-Lies-Bleeding (*Amaranthus caudatus*), Moss Rose (*Rosa centifolia*), Nasturtium (*Tropaeolum*), Petunia (*Petunia* sp.), Spider Flower (*Cleome hasslerana*), Sweet Alyssum (*Lobularia maritima*), Sweet-Sultan (*Centaurea moschata*)

FLOWERS THAT TOLERATE ACID SOIL

Annuals: Calliopsis (*Calliopsis tinctoria*), Flowering Tobacco (*Nicotiana alata*), Marigold (*Tagetes* sp.), Verbena (*Verbena* sp.)

FLOWERS THAT TOLERATE ALKALINE SOIL

Annuals: Candytuft (*Iberis* sp.), Corn Poppy (*Papaver rhoeas*), Drummond Phlox (*Phlox drummondii*), Impatiens or Garden Balsam (*Impatiens balsamina*), Mignonette (*Reseda* sp.), Nasturtium (*Tropaeolum* sp.), Zinnia (*Zinnia* sp.)

Perennials: Baptisia (*Baptisia* sp.), Coreopsis (*Coreopsis tinctoria*), Gypsophilia (*Gypsophilia* sp.), Hollyhock (*Alcea* sp.), Iris (*Iris* sp.), Japanese Anemone (*Anemone hupehensis*), Silene (*Silene* sp.)

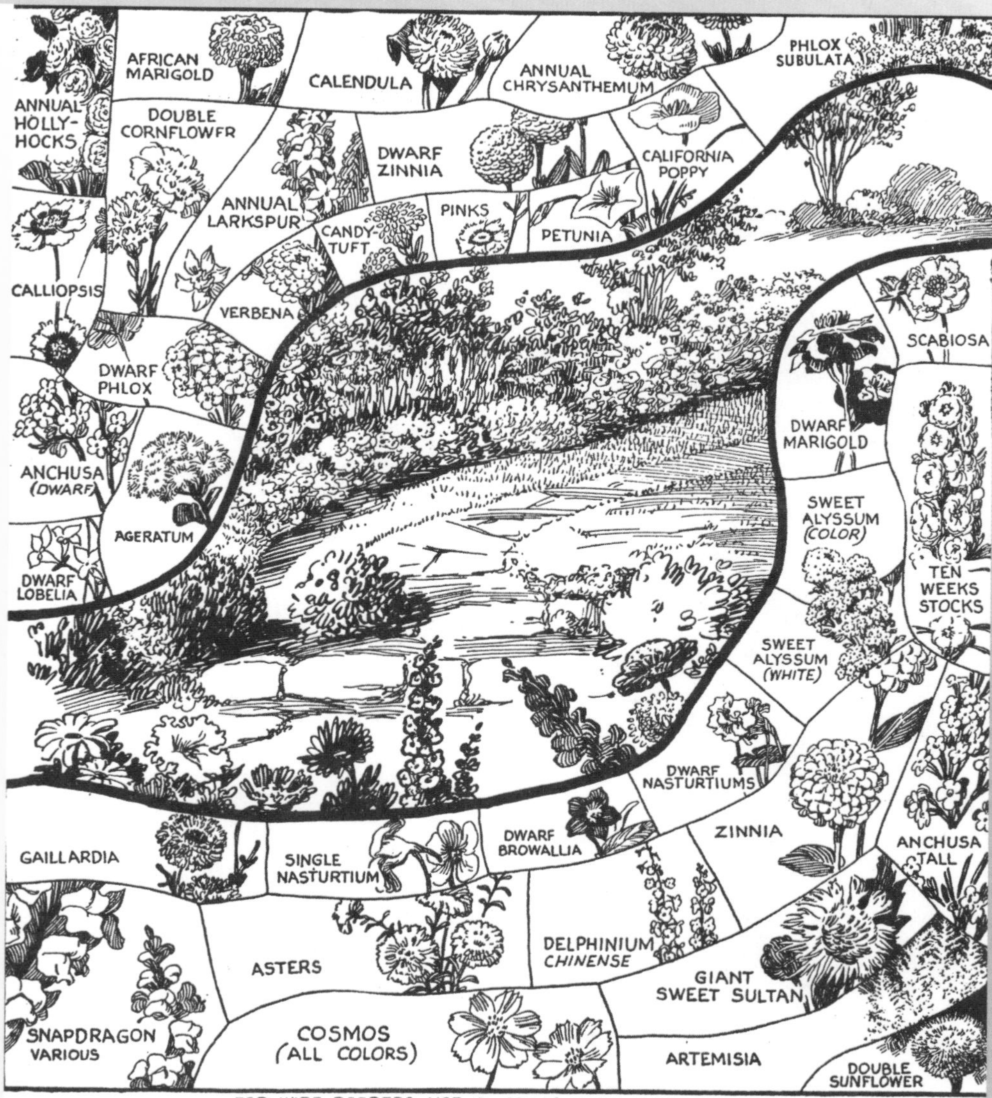

FLOWERS THAT TOLERATE HEAT AND DROUGHT

Annuals: Calliopsis (*Calliopsis tinctoria*), Cape Marigold (*Dimorphotheca* sp.), Cornflower or Bachelor's Button (*Centaurea cyanus*), Drummond Phlox (*Phlox drummondii*), Four-O'clock (*Mirabilis jalapa*), Green Perilla (*Perilla frutescens*), Larkspur (*Consolida* sp.), Morning Glory (*Ipomoea* sp.), Moss Rose (*Rosa centifolia*), Sanvitalia (*Sanvitalia procumbens*), Scarlet Sage (*Salvia coccinea*), Showy Pricklepoppy (*Argemone grandiflora*), Snow on the Mountain (*Euphorbia marginata*), Summer Cypress (*Kochia scoparia*), Sunflower (*Helianthus annuus*), Zinnia (*Zinnia* sp.)

FOR WIDE BORDERS USE A GRASS WALK ALONG THE REAR

The sketch above shows a well-thought-out plan for two flower beds divided by a grassy walkway. The gardener has observed the tallest-to-the-rear rule and balanced color nicely, without creating an artificial or overly planned look. The flowers chosen are easy to grow, and even the perennials will bloom in the first season. Notice the inclusion of annuals that can be transplanted or resown to fill in gaps that occur in late summer when perennials go dormant.

GIANT VELVET MIXED SALPIGLOSSIS
THE 9 PACKETS FOR 50 cts.

Flowers are usually discussed in terms of annuals—plants that last only one season and do not survive winter—and perennials, plants that last several seasons.

Annuals

However, the dividing lines between these two classes are not as sharply drawn as one might think, and if you read from several garden books you are likely to become confused. For example, some plants are annuals but are so efficient at reseeding themselves they may be referred to as "perennials" when it comes to planning a garden. There are also biennials, which grow

for two seasons. Most biennials spend their first season producing stems and leaves, and it is only in the second season that the plant blooms, produces seed, and dies. Common biennials include Canterbury bells, foxglove, some species of forget-me-nots, English daisies, hollyhocks, pansies, wallflower, and sweet William. Because their lives are brief and plants purchased from a nursery are already in their blooming season, they are generally discussed and handled as if they were annuals. If you are sowing biennials from seed, sow every year so that you will always have a crop coming into bloom.

Annuals are indispensable in the home garden. They are easy to care for and cultivate and come in a wide variety of colors, types of foliage, and sizes. While most prefer open, sunny locations and good garden loam, there are species that will tolerate everything from shade to poor, alkaline, or acidic soil. (See the specialized lists, pages 63–65). The chief advantage of annuals is that they are continuous bloomers, excellent for taking up the slack after spring's tulips have faded and capable of blooming through the heat of summer, after many perennials have fallen. If season-round color and an abundance of blooms to cut for indoor display are desired, consider stocking your garden with a wide variety of annuals.

PREPARING THE SOIL

For most annuals, ideal soil is nothing more exotic than a good garden loam with a pH of 6.5 to 7.5. Soil need only be cultivated once a year, either in the fall or early spring. While double digging (see page 32) is best and should be done at least every several years, a simpler method can be used in intervening seasons. To cultivate, spread soil with a layer of well-rotted manure or good compost and work in with a fork or spade. If this is done in spring, the soil should be broken into fine particles and raked level. If done in the autumn, leave the surface of the soil rough through the winter, then break and rake prior to spring planting.

RAISING SEEDLINGS

Annuals are almost always grown from seed, and who among us has not been tempted by the lush, colorful blooms beckoning from seed packets? Nevertheless, many people opt for nursery plants because the areas they live in don't provide a long enough growing season for their favorite annuals to flower if they sow them directly into the soil. However, starting seedlings indoors can be extremely rewarding and does not require expensive equipment or special lights. Here's how old-timers raised seedlings in the days when no gardeners worth their salt would think of going to a nursery for "ready made" plants:

1. Indoor sowing should begin one month to six weeks before you anticipate outdoor planting.
2. Fancy containers are not needed. If you are planting a small number of seeds, a large clay flower pot will do. For larger numbers, a shallow wooden box or nine-by-thirteen-inch metal cake pan with numerous holes punched into the bottom (with nail and hammer) work well.

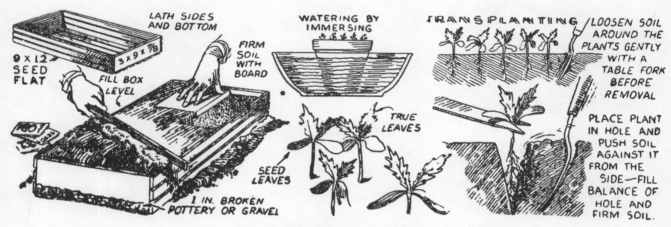

PLANTING SEEDS INDOORS

3. To prepare a flower pot, place several large stones or pieces of broken pot or crockery in the bottom and cover with one to two inches of coarse gravel. (If the pot is new, it should be soaked in water for a few days beforehand.) Fill the container with good potting soil or a homemade mixture of equal parts garden loam, clean sand, and humus. Make sure this mixture is finely broken up and free of debris. Use another pot to pack down the soil and fill to about one inch from the top. Now water the soil by setting the pot in room-temperature water that is about two-thirds the depth of the pot. When dampness appears on the surface of the soil, remove it from the water and set aside for an hour or so to allow a bit of drying.
4. A box should be prepared in much the same way as a pot, with initial layers of large stones or broken pottery, and gravel covered with conditioned soil. Because boxes of wood and metal are not as porous as a clay pot, you will need to water the soil as you add it, being careful not to add so much water that the soil becomes flooded and muddy. If you are raising delicate seeds that require extra warmth, a piece of glass can be placed over the top and

SOWING SMALL SEEDS

shaded with a piece of newspaper. Just remember to raise one end of the glass at least one-quarter inch to allow air to circulate, and place the box out of harm's way.

5. Place seeds in the prepared container, and cover with a layer of fine soil. The rule of thumb is to make this layer three times as deep as the seed's circumference. Very small seeds can be pressed into the soil and not covered at all, except with a piece of paper to prevent them from drying out.

6. Be sure to label the pots as you go. Plant only one species in each and mark accordingly. Seeds in boxes should be planted in rows, and each row should be clearly labeled.

7. While germinating, seeds should be kept at about 70 degrees F., and should not be placed in the sun. The biggest risk to germinating seeds is that they will dry out. To prevent this, a piece of paper or cloth placed over the container is recommended. If the soil becomes too dry, water it gently.

PRICKING OFF SEEDLINGS

8. When plants begin to germinate, the container should be moved to a location that receives good indirect light. If possible, find a place that is somewhat cool—about 50 to 60 degrees F. This will promote hardy seedlings that will do well when transplanted.

9. Water seedlings cautiously. The plant should be kept somewhat dry and should not be allowed to get too wet, as this promotes damping-off, a fungal condition caused by too much moisture and not enough ventilation. If your soil is prone to wetness, add sand to the mix.

WATERING SEEDS OR SEEDLINGS

10. As seedlings grow, it will be necessary to thin them out. When you do this, be sure to remove the entire plant, rather than breaking it off, as the roots left behind will compete with the plants you have chosen to keep. Thin once and, if growth seems sluggish, thin again.

11. Keep seedlings out of direct sunlight until they are well-leafed and several inches high, then harden the seedlings gradually by continuing to shade them from the brightest sun.

12. Wait to transplant seedlings until their first true leaves have flowered (not to be confused with the seed leaves, which appear first). However, once the true leaves show, feel free to transplant seedlings to roomier pots and trays. Contrary to popular myth, this actually helps young plants develop hardiness.

13. Well-developed seedlings may be further hardened by setting them outside during the day and bringing them in at night.

—adapted from *The Modern Family Garden Book*, 1941

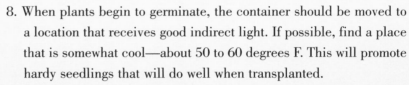
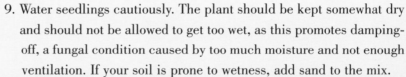
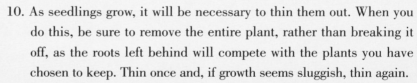
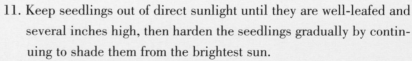
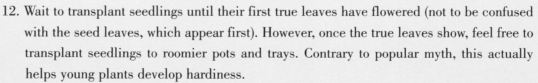
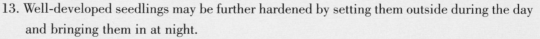

PLANTING OUT SEEDLINGS

PINCHING BACK

Some annuals should be pinched back when they are young to prevent them from developing a spindly look with few blooms. To do this, wait until two or three sets of true leaves have developed, then nip the terminal bud (tip of the plant) just above the next highest set of leaves. This will cause side shoots to develop, giving the plant a fuller look with more blooms.

SETTING OUT PLANTS

Have you ever watched a successful gardener set out new plants? It is a fascinating experience and one not easily forgotten. What a joy it is to watch the concentration, the swift precision, the delicacy in handling tiny plants, and the loving care with which the work is done! The successful gardener has learned from experience that results from new plants depend, to a great extent, on how they are set out.

—*The Home Garden*, May 1945

For most gardeners, planting is the single most satisfying activity to do, and following a few simple guidelines will ensure the best results. First, remember that you don't have to put plants into the soil the day you buy them, or the day you intended to plant them. If the chosen day is too cold or too hot, or if the ground is soggy, it's better to wait for more favorable conditions. Keep plants waiting in a cool, well-ventilated place and they'll be fine. The best time to plant is in the late afternoon if it is spring and the early evening if it is summer. This gives the plants a long, cool night in which to revive before facing the sun's rays. While planting, keep roots covered with damp cloth or earth until you are actually ready to place the plant in the soil. Even a few minutes of exposure to air and light can be drying. As you add dirt around the plant, be sure to pack it down with your hands. A loosely set plant will not become well-established, and may be uprooted by rain. After the plant is placed snugly in its new home, thoroughly wet the soil around the plant. Cover the damp soil with a fine layer of dirt or moss to prevent it from drying.

GENERAL CARE TIPS

For best results, soil around annuals should be well-weeded and frequently worked with a hand cultivator to keep soil fine and loose. A layer of summer mulch or peat moss is also advisable in hot, dry months, as most annuals prefer cool, moist soil. Removing fading blossoms is especially important for annuals, which stop blooming once they have gone to seed, and will greatly prolong their productive period. If soil needs to be enriched, a commercial fertilizer of 4-12-4 can be applied in July and again in early August—just be careful not to get any on the foliage or blooms.

There are far too many species of annuals to list, but here just a few that are definitely worth your consideration.

- **ANNUAL PINKS** (*Dianthus* sp.): As the name implies, this plant is devoted to a single color range—yet within it you will find everything from white to salmon, scarlet, and deep crimson, in single as well as double varieties. Pinks prefer a sunny location and rich, moist soil, and should not be planted outdoors until the soil has warmed.

CALENDULA Variety : CAMPFIRE

- **CALENDULA** (*Calendula officinalis*): The calendula's orange or yellow blossoms are a favorite for cutting gardens, because they are easy to grow and they hold up well after cutting. Seeds can be sown outdoors in spring when the ground is workable, or started indoors and transplanted.
- **CORNFLOWER OR BACHELOR'S BUTTONS** (*Centaurea cyanus*): One of the easiest flowers to grow, cornflowers will flourish even in poor soil and require very little care. Seeds can be sown in autumn (to lie dormant through the winter) or at any time during the spring when the soil is work able. Because the blooming period of each plant is short, successive sowings should be made.

- **IMPATIENS** (*Impatiens balsamina*): Also known as garden balsam, impatiens is one of the few flowering plants that tolerate—and even prefer—lots of shade. So long as the soil is kept moist, these plants will produce profuse blooms from spring until frost strikes and, once started, require little care. Nurseries produce such hardy examples of this species at such reasonable prices, it's worth the few dollars to buy well-started plants and begin enjoying the blooms right away.

LARKSPUR
Variety : TALL BRANCHING MIXED

- **LARKSPUR** (*Consolida* sp.): Valued by gardeners for their height (three to four feet) and dramatic spires of bloom, larkspur comes in a range of colors, from white to shell pink and vivid purple. Seeds must be sown in late autumn or in spring, as soon as the ground is workable; plants started at other times will not flourish. As long as they are sown at appropriate times, larkspur grows vigorously and is exceptionally hardy. If you have a greenhouse, larkspur makes a good year-round cutting flower.
- **MARIGOLD** (*Tagetes* sp.): If you think you can't grow anything, try marigolds. This unfussy plant can tolerate poor soil and thrive in almost any conditions—in full sun or partial shade, and in wet conditions or dry. They are so rugged they can even be successfully transplanted when they are flowering. Bright and generous bloomers, marigolds can be counted on to flower from mid-summer until the first frost. Seeds, which can be sown outdoors or started indoors, are large and easy to handle, and an excellent choice if you have young children who want to plant seeds of their own.
- **PETUNIA** (*Petunia* sp.): Like the marigold, the petunia is a hardy plant that will thrive in a variety of conditions. Gardeners value it not only for its sturdiness but for its versatility—it grows well in the ground, pots, window boxes, and hanging baskets. Its blooming period is longer than most other flowers and it comes in a staggering variety of shapes—single, double, ruffled, and fluted—and colors. The only it presents is a tendency to become spindly, but this is easily remedied by pruning the plant.

MANDEVILLE Triple-Tested FLOWER SEEDS assure You of a Beautiful Garden

More than 70,000 Retail Stores offer You this CONVENIENT, MODERN WAY to select your Triple-Tested Seeds

- **SNAPDRAGON** (*Antirrhinum* sp.): What child hasn't delighted in squeezing the cheeks of this blossom to make the dragon open its mouth? Valued for the clear, vivid colors of its blooms, which come in shades of pink, apricot, tawny yellow, and deep red, this plant is a bit difficult to start from seed but, once established, it can grow in a variety of conditions. If sown from seed, plants should be started indoors or in outdoor cold frames (see "Build a Cold Frame," page 121), to be transplanted outdoors when soil becomes warm and workable. It is important to pinch back developing plants to encourage branching, and to remove fading blossoms from mature plants to ensure continuous bloom. In warm climates, the plant will live through the winter and can be treated as a perennial.

SWEET ALYSSUM
Variety : SNOW CARPET

- **SWEET ALYSSUM** (*Lobularia maritima*): Low to the ground and loaded with delicate, frothy blossoms, sweet alyssum is a popular and durable plant, perfect for edging a flower bed or walkway. Alyssum can be sown outdoors as soon as the frost is out of the ground. Seedlings grow rapidly and blossom within six weeks of planting.

- **ZINNIA** (*Zinnia* sp.): Like the cornflower, the zinnia can be counted on to succeed when all else fails. It will endure both drought and outright neglect, which may be one reason why it is among the most popular of all garden flowers. Zinnias bloom from mid-summer through autumn, produce large vivid flowers that come in a broad range of colors and sizes, and will survive transplanting even when in full flower. Seeds can be sown outside when all danger of frost has passed, or started indoors and transplanted. While the common zinnia prefers full sun, there are also varieties that do well in partial shade.

Although it may seem that perennials require little care because they don't need to be planted yearly, this isn't true. Perennials simply require a different kind of care. Learn the basics, and your perennials will repay your efforts year after year.

Perennials

Like annuals, most perennials prefer neutral soil that has a pH of 6.5 to 7.5. Because soil changes over time, it is a good idea to test the soil every few years in the spring and, if necessary, correct the balance. In the spring, after mulch has been removed (see "Winter Protection," page 78), check perennials to see if any have been heaved up by freezing and thawing, and then

press them firmly back into the soil. At this time, all dead stalks and leaves should be removed (a task that should also be done in the fall), as well as any debris left by winter. As soon as the soil is warm and dry enough to work, it should be cultivated. It is desirable to double dig the soil every four to six seasons, a large task but one well worth the effort. (Directions for correcting pH levels and for double digging are found in "Soil: The Key Ingredient.") If you have large numbers of perennials, double dig in sections, doing one section each season, to keep the workload manageable. Double digging can be done in either the spring or fall, though many gardeners prefer fall because it is convenient for planting new bulbs and dividing old ones. Most plants can be lifted out of the soil and set aside with their roots carefully covered while the work goes on but fussy perennials such as peonies and bleeding heart, which don't like to be disturbed, can be left in the ground and carefully worked around. Soil not being re-conditioned, or soil that was dug in the fall, should be worked in the spring with a hand cultivator to break up clumps and reduce soil to a fine texture.

PERENNIAL WATER NEEDS

Unless you live in an arid region or are going through a drought, your perennials may not need additional watering on your part, as the majority of these plants require the kind of moderate moisture supplied by natural rainfall. If you do need to water, avoid light, frequent waterings which do nothing but bring the feeding roots to the surface. Instead, water thoroughly every four or five days, providing enough moisture to penetrate the ground to a depth of at least one foot. Watering in the late afternoon or early evening is best, as it will prevent rapid evaporation.

WHEN TO FERTILIZE

Two treatments with commercial fertilizer (4-12-4 or 4-8-6) each season will keep your perennials healthy and well fed (follow package directions). The first application should be made in spring, after the plants have started their active growth cycle, and the second should be made in early summer. Avoid fertilizing in late summer and fall as this can stimulate growth and send the plant into winter in an immature condition.

PERENNIALS FROM SEED

Perennials can be grown from seed just as annuals can. However, spring sowing is not necessarily the rule with perennials as it is with annuals. Study the requirements of the species you're starting before you begin. When it's time to transplant seedlings, many gardeners prefer to place them in an outdoor nursery bed first, and move them to their permanent location in fall. This allows the gardener to select only the healthiest, best-established specimens for permanent planting.

DIVIDING PERENNIALS

"Perennial" doesn't mean "eternal." Many perennials grow so rampantly that they will flag after a few seasons unless they are dug up and divided. Not all perennials fall into this category, though. Peonies, for example, don't like to be disturbed and will grow quite happily in the same spot for twenty years or even longer. Oriental poppy, bleeding heart, and Japanese anemone also do best with rare, infrequent resetting. Hardy chrysanthemums, on the other hand, will choke themselves with new growth unless attended to. A good way to tell which plants need to be divided is simply to look at their bases. Typically you will see a ring of live growth surrounding a dead, depleted center, or a pattern in which the crowding shoots seem to be literally lifting the plant up and out of the soil. Once you've decided which plants need attention, follow these steps for a successful operation:

1. Choose the right time of year. The best time to divide a perennial is after the plant flowers and goes into its dormant stage. The month and season for this work will vary depending both on the species of plant and climate you live in. Plants that bloom late into the year, such as hardy mums, should be allowed to rest over the winter and be divided in the spring.

2. Before digging, draw a plan of the flower bed as you would like it to appear after the operation is completed. This way, you will know where the divided plants should be replanted. If you are going to move some of the newly divided plants to other parts of your garden, decide where now.

3. Another important thing to do before beginning the actual dividing work is to tag each plant with a label. This may seem unnecessary, but once trimmed down and removed from their familiar spots, you may easily confuse one plant with another.

4. Cut off the tops with pruning shears, leaving only four to five inches of stem.

Catalogue of Seeds for 1929

DEPOSIT SEED CO.
DEPOSIT, N.Y.

A WONDERFUL
DOLLAR
COLLECTION
OF
DELPHINIUMS

5. If the plant does not have an extensive root system, remove the entire plant from the ground. Perennials with large and matted root systems, such as helianthus, must be dug in sections, using the spade to cut through tangled roots.

6. Set the plants aside, covering their roots.

7. Once the plants are removed, go through the soil to remove broken root ends and other debris. Then mix in a good amount of compost or shredded peat moss. A commercial fertilizer should also be added.

8. Small, loosely connected plant clumps can be divided by gently breaking them apart with your hands or cutting vertically through the clump with a knife. A spade can be used to cut through larger clumps. How many pieces a plant should be divided into depends on its size and health. A vigorous plant that measures about one foot in diameter will easily give you four healthy fledglings. Make sure each new plant has at least one healthy growing stalk.

9. Plant as usual, taking care to dig the hole deep enough so that the roots aren't folded or jammed in.

—adapted from *The Home Garden*, October 1944

WINTER PROTECTION

Perennials that carry their leaves over the winter do not require special protection. Others will profit from a properly applied winter mulch. Many people want to take care of their perennials by giving them a good, snug blanket for the winter; however this does more harm than good. Many perennials do need winter protection, but packing them with material will smother them and cause them to heat up too early in the spring. For plants, the chief danger of winter is not from cold but from unexpected warm spells. These periods are inevitably followed by a return to cold, causing warming and refreezing that is damaging to plants.

Straw and hardwood leaves, which are slow to decay, make a good winter mulch but even these must be applied in a way that will prevent them from becoming packed or sodden (this will smother the plants). The best plan is to wait until the ground is frozen solid, then erect a small structure around the plant that will prevent the mulch from packing down around it—a chicken wire cage, over and around which the mulch is placed, works well. Plants native to warmer climates may need more protection. In this case, a box or basket of loose leaves inverted over the plant will provide protection yet keep out the moisture that turns mulch into a heavy, sodden mass.

FIVE FAVORITE PERENNIALS

Every gardener should be familiar with the five indispensable perennials listed below. These flowers are propagated by seed. For perennials propagated from bulbs, such as tulips, see Chapter 8 "Bulbs and Their Cousins," page 81.

- **DAYLILY** (*Hemerocallis* sp.): Not to be confused with the lily, which grows from a bulb, the daylily is one of the most versatile perennials around, coming in a variety of shapes and sizes, and a dramatic array of single- and double-toned shades. Daylilies can be planted any time when the soil is workable, though fall is best. They will grow in almost any location that gives six hours of daily sun, and bloom happily from late spring until autumn. They are also able to tolerate drought, and are particularly pest-resistant.

- **GERANIUM** (*Geranium* sp.): A true perennial in its native South Africa, the geranium cannot survive frost and is best treated as an annual or brought indoors in regions where "winter" is more than a state of mind. Other than this caveat, geraniums require little care, needing six or more hours of sunlight a day and medium-rich, well-drained soil. They will do well in the garden, or in pots, window boxes, and hanging baskets.

- **LILY-OF-THE-VALLEY** (*Convallaria majalis*): Perhaps one of the most heavenly scented of all flowers, the lily-of-the-valley is invaluable for those with cool, shady spots to fill. This location, a no-grow zone for most plants, is this flower's ideal spot. With its tiny, bell-shaped blossoms, the lily-of-the-valley may seem delicate, but is rarely afflicted by pests or diseases, and requires little care once it is planted. Although a true perennial with a life span of several years, the lily of the valley prefers a cool climate, and will die in areas with hot summers.

- **PHLOX** (*Phlox* sp.): If you want a mosaic of color without the trouble of mixing species, try phlox. The plant comes in a range of colors that combine well, from forget-me-not blue to vibrant magenta. Phlox do well in full sunlight but will also tolerate partial shade, and bloom from June through early September, when many other perennials have faded. One other reason to try phlox—their lovely fragrance attracts butterflies.

- **PRIMROSE** (*Primula* sp.): These come in a variety of flower shapes and shades, and are notable because they prefer full to partial shade. Most varieties also prefer acidic soil with a pH of 5.5 to 6.5. They don't do well in hot climates or dry soil, but if you have the right conditions, these dainty little flowers should be at the top of your list.

WINTER PROTECTION

AFTER A GOOD FREEZE A NETWORK OF CORN STALKS OR BRUSH WILL KEEP LEAF MULCH FROM SMOTHERING THE PLANTS

A CIRCLE OF WIRE NETTING 6 IN. HIGH, WILL KEEP COVERS AWAY FROM PLANTS HAVING WINTER FOLIAGE AND KEEP MULCH ON SURROUNDING GROUND

TO AVOID DECAY—PUT A SHOVEL OR TWO OF COAL ASHES AROUND DELPHINIUMS AFTER THE COLD WEATHER STARTS.

USE A PANE OF GLASS FOR THE MANY ALPINES AND OTHER PLANTS THAT NEED PROTECTION AGAINST MOISTURE.

After a long winter, or even a short one, no sight is so welcome as that of the tips of the first daffodils peeking above the ground. These favorites belong to a class of perennials that are known, to laypeople, as bulbs. In fact, this class is made up of three different types of plants—bulbs, corms (which resemble bulbs), and tubers (which resemble fleshy, engorged roots). To the home gardener, there is little practical difference between a true bulb,

Bulbs AND THEIR COUSINS

which has overlapping scales or layers, and the corm, which is a single, solid mass. The lily, for example, grows from a true bulb, while gladiolus grows from a corm. The dahlia, which many people may also refer to as a bulb, is actually a tuber.

BULBS AND SHRUBS

One advantage in planting bulbs beneath the shelter of shrubs is that they can remain where they are after flowering. Usually the place is not needed for summer-blooming plants and the shrub foliage soon becomes dense enough to hide the leaves and stems of the bulb plants before they become unsightly. They should not be cut off while still green.

The same is true when small groupings of tulips, narcissus, or other bulbs are placed here and there in a perennial border. The foliage can go right on growing and maturing for the development of the next year's bulbs until it naturally dies down in June or July. Meanwhile, the taller plantsare coming up around them to hide the yellowing leaves.

—*Better Homes & Gardens*, September 1934

PLANNING AND LOCATION

Many people think that all plants in the bulb category are spring bloomers but this isn't the case. There are early spring bloomers and late spring bloomers, as well as those that do not bloom until summer. It's also helpful to remember that bulb-type plants also come in a variety of heights, from dainty hyacinths to towering lilies. Before purchasing your favorites, list the bulbs by their mature height and projected blooming times. This will help you plan for a well-proportioned, continuous show of flowers.

Some extra thought also needs to go into where you are going to locate your plants. You want to plant them where they will bloom, as transplanting is not recommended once bulbs begin to root. If you plan to use your bulbs again, you will want to let them die back rather than lifting them or removing the foliage. During this process, plants often become extremely unattractive, so you will want to mix them with plants that will improve the view.

BULB SOIL

The three bulbous types are alike in one respect. They all need deep cultivation and thorough drainage. Cold stiff clay soil may rot them. Moisture may be held for them by a liberal supply of peat; all types like it.

—*The Complete Book of Garden Magic*, 1935

With the exception of a few varieties of iris that actually prefer damp locales, rot is the ever-present enemy of every bulb, corm, and tuber. For this reason, extra care must be taken to ensure good drainage. Prepare the soil by digging to a depth of two feet. The bottom foot should drain thoroughly. If this is not happening, place a three-inch layer of cinders or gravel at the very bottom of the hole. The upper foot should be a rich, sandy loam, moist yet free of stagnant water. An excellent old-timer's preparation is to mix the topsoil with peat moss, then add about one handful of

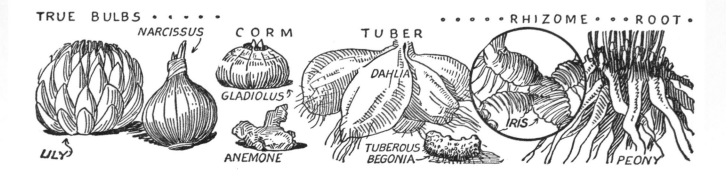

ground bone meal, one handful of steamed bone meal, and two handfuls of wood ashes per square yard. Well-rotted manure should be avoided at this point. If you wish to use it, begin in spring by mixing it with soil, forking it over several times during the summer, then breaking it up finely or sifting it through a coarse screen for use in the fall.

GETTING THE BEST BLOOMS

Like all perennials, bulbous plants must be dealt with year-round.

- **PLANTING:** Different bulbs have different planting schedules. Spring bloomers should be planted in autumn to give the root system time to develop. Narcissus, crocus, bulb iris, snowdrops, spring snowflakes, and winter aconite should be planted in early autumn, while tulips, hyacinths, and scillas can be planted later. Summer bloomers are generally planted in the spring or even summer, depending on the species. The biggest risk in planting is placing the bulbs too near the surface. It is better to plant too deep than too shallow. How deep to plant them depends on the species. An old rule of thumb is that the top of the bulb should be covered with soil that is three times as deep as the bulb's diameter at its widest point. The second risk in planting is creating air pockets, which can promote rot. To guard against this, firm the soil before setting the bulb, and press the bulb down into the soil. Then fill in, firming the soil along the way. After planting, a thorough watering will stimulate root growth.

- **WINTER MULCH:** Mulching should be done after the ground has frozen, otherwise damp may set in. Another reason to wait for cold weather is to keep mice from selecting your mulch as their winter quarters—a snug den for them but a disappointment for you when, come spring, you discover they have nibbled the tender shoots right down to the ground. Once the ground has frozen thoroughly, cover plants with four to six inches of hardwood leaves or clean wheat straw held in place with stakes or wire netting. When spring arrives, check the mulch to make sure it is still light and dry and, if it is, leave in place until all danger of frost has passed. This will protect your plants from frost as well as from premature growth.

- **AFTER BLOOMING:** After the bulb has bloomed, the top growth must be allowed to mature three to five weeks if the bulb is to develop and bloom again the next season. It is important not to trim the wilting foliage or dig up the bulb during this time, but to allow it to complete its natural cycle. If you plan to move the bulbs, the best time to do this is as soon as this cycle is complete and the top of the plant has thoroughly dried. The reason: some bulbs begin to develop a new root system almost immediately, and moving them once this has begun can cause root damage. Once bulbs are carefully dug, discard any that are soft or small and get the remaining stock into appropriate containers as soon as possible, because exposure to air can be damaging. Keep them in trays of peat, dry sand, or sawdust until they are needed, and make sure they do not become damp.

A QUICK GUIDE TO POPULAR BULBS

Bulbs, corms, and tubers come in such a dazzling array it's worth it to try these easy-to-grow plants. Here are some especially beautiful varieties.

SPRING BLOOMERS

- **CROCUS** (*Crocus* sp.): This is an inexpensive and reliable bulb that looks especially good in mass plantings. Though most people think of the classic purple variety, crocus also comes in paper white, cream yellow, and copper. Crocus multiplies quickly and, if not dug up, will reward you with larger clumps of bloom each year.

- **GLORY-OF-THE-SNOW** (*Chionodoxa* sp.): With its spear-shaped petals that radiate outward, the blossom of this plant resembles a bright little star with a white center and heavenly blue, lavender, or magenta tips. The plant gets its name from its exceptionally early appearance, often seeming to push up through the snow. Because of this, the bulbs can be planted under trees and still get the sun they need.

- **GRAPE HYACINTH** (*Muscari botryoides*): Not to be confused with the hyacinth, which is a larger plant, grape hyacinth is distinguished by its stalk of tiny, bell-shaped flowers that resemble a cluster of grapes. This plant is not fussy or temperamental, and will grow well even in somewhat gritty soil.

- **HYACINTH** (*Hyacinthus* sp.): Valued for their lavish, stately flower stalks and delightful perfume, hyacinths come in a wide variety of shades, from white to yellow, pink, blue, purple, and even orange. Unlike some spring bulbs, whose blooming period is relatively short, hyacinths will stay crisp and fresh-looking for two or three weeks.

- **IRIS** (*Iris* sp.): This large flower family consists of over two hundred different species, not all of which form tubers and not all of which bloom in spring. Whether spring or summer bloomers, irises generally prefer full sun, and most are prolific growers. When a clump begins to bloom poorly, usually after four or five years of growth, it should be divided. Although different species require somewhat different handling, tuberous irises are divided by separating portions of the rhizome, or tuber. Notice the points marked A, B, and C in the illustration, (top, opposite page), and how the tuber cosists of bulges connectedby thin necks. What you want to do is discard the old growth—C in the illustration—and create new and vigorous plants by separating at the thin neck points. While it is acceptable to do this by breaking off each bulge—separating at the A points—you will get stronger plants if you divide at the B points in the illustration, leaving several of the bulges together to form a vigorous new clump.

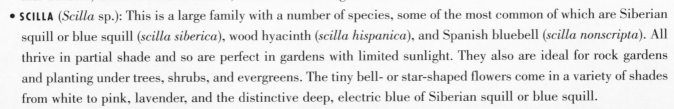

HOW TO DIVIDE THE RHIZOMES WHEN RESETTING THE OLD CLUMPS OF IRIS.

- **NARCISSUS** (*Narcissus* sp.): This is another large family of plants that includes a number of familiar friends, such as numerous varieties of narcissi, daffodils, and jonquils. The flowers are yellow or white, or a combination of the two, with the central cup of one shade surrounded by petals in the other. In addition to their beauty, these plants are virtually foolproof. They grow well in sun or partial shade and can be planted in perennial borders, under trees and shrubs, or scattered throughout the lawn itself.

- **SCILLA** (*Scilla* sp.): This is a large family with a number of species, some of the most common of which are Siberian squill or blue squill (*scilla siberica*), wood hyacinth (*scilla hispanica*), and Spanish bluebell (*scilla nonscripta*). All thrive in partial shade and so are perfect in gardens with limited sunlight. They also are ideal for rock gardens and planting under trees, shrubs, and evergreens. The tiny bell- or star-shaped flowers come in a variety of shades from white to pink, lavender, and the distinctive deep, electric blue of Siberian squill or blue squill.

- **SNOWDROP** (*Galanthus* sp.): Like the glory-of-the-snow, this bulb owes its name to its early bloom as much as to its white, teardrop-shaped petals. Snowdrops prefer moist soil and partial shade, and should be planted in large numbers for the loveliest effect.

- **TULIP** (*Tulipa* sp.): The monarch of bulb-type plants, the tulip hardly needs an introduction. A native of Turkey, the plant is most often associated with the Netherlands, where prices once soared to thousands of dollars and created one of the greatest speculative bubbles in history. Today, they are within the reach of every home gardener. Tulips are easy to bring to bloom and will grow in almost any type of soil, provided it is well drained. They are the last bulb to be planted in fall and need cold weather to return year after year. In warm climates, which will not chill them properly, they are best treated as annuals. Today's tulips come in many variations of height, color, and flower shape—from short to tall, solid to variegated shades, single to double petaled, and ruffled to fringed. They also come in early-, mid-, and late-blooming varieties, allowing the true enthusiast to enjoy them from April through late May.

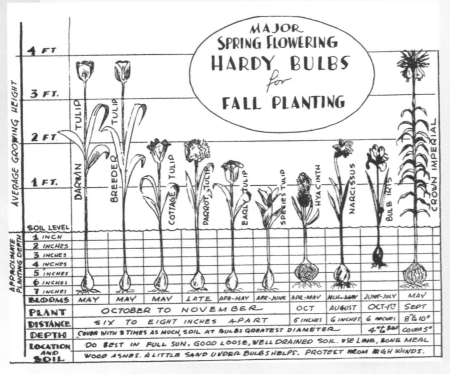

MAJOR SPRING FLOWERING HARDY BULBS for FALL PLANTING

	DARWIN TULIP	BREEDER TULIP	COTTAGE TULIP	PARROT TULIP	EARLY TULIP	SPECIES TULIP	HYACINTH	NARCISSUS	BULB IRIS	CROWN IMPERIAL
BLOOMS	MAY	MAY	MAY	LATE	APR-MAY	APR-JUNE	APR-MAY	MCH-MAY	JUNE-JULY	MAY
PLANT	OCTOBER TO NOVEMBER						OCT	AUGUST	OCT-1ST	SEPT
DISTANCE	SIX TO EIGHT INCHES APART						5 INCHES	6 INCHES	6 INCHES	8"-10"
DEPTH	COVER WITH 3 TIMES AS MUCH SOIL AT BULBS GREATEST DIAMETER								4"-6" BAR	COVER 5"
LOCATION AND SOIL	DO BEST IN FULL SUN. GOOD LOOSE, WELL DRAINED SOIL. USE LIME, BONE MEAL WOOD ASHES. A LITTLE SAND UNDER BULBS HELPS. PROTECT FROM HIGH WINDS.									

AVERAGE GROWING HEIGHT: 4 FT., 3 FT., 2 FT., 1 FT.

APPROXIMATE PLANTING DEPTH: SOIL LEVEL, 1 INCH, 2 INCHES, 3 INCHES, 4 INCHES, 5 INCHES, 6 INCHES, 7 INCHES

- **WINTER ACONITE** (*Eranthis* sp.): This low-growing plant has a sun-yellow flower reminiscent of a buttercup. It blooms extremely early and, though its flowering period is relatively short, forms an attractive green ground cover after the blooms die. Winter aconite will tolerate full sun in cool climates only; elsewhere, it does best in partial shade, and must be watered when there is little rainfall to keep the tubers from drying out.

SUMMER BLOOMERS

- **BEGONIA** (*Begonia* sp.): A South African native, the begonia is actually a large category of flowering plants, but the tuberous variety most of us are familiar with is a hybrid cultured from numerous species. Despite their tropical origins, begonias are not difficult to grow, requiring only good drainage and able to thrive in partial shade. These plants cannot survive winter, so they either need to be treated as annuals or dug up two weeks before the first expected frost. To do this, remove all dying stems and leaves to prevent rot. Dig up the plants, leaving some soil attached. Clean off the soil and store tubers in trays, layered in peat or vermiculite, in a cool, dry place until spring. When the tops have wilted, remove them. With their large single- or double-petaled flowers and variety of sizes and hues, begonias are well worth trying.

- **DAHLIA** (*Dahlia pinnata*): Dahlias come in a wide range of shapes, with varieties that resemble everything from daisies to peonies and spider mums. Like begonias, dahlias are not winter hardy and should not be planted until spring, when all danger of frost is past. Blooming vigor can be improved by pinching back the tips of the main stems three weeks after planting and removing faded blooms. Dig tubers in fall and store over winter. Divide and plant in spring, discarding tubers which have broken crowns, as new plants will not grow from them.

- **GLADIOLUS** (*Gladiolus* sp.): When the rest of the garden begins to look a bit wan and ragged, count on gladiolus to liven things up. With their tall, blossom-laden spires and brilliant hues, these plants bloom from mid-summer through autumn. They can be planted as late as June, will still flower before frost, and will grow in almost any type of well-drained, sunny spot. Their leaves, stems, and flowers are unusually crisp and hold up well when cut. To divide gladiolus, dig the plant when the leaves begin to brown and allow them to wither completely. You will notice small bulblets, or cormels, attached to the main corm. Remove stalks and leaves when they are fully withered and no more green can be seen. Leave cormels attached to corms and store in trays in dry sand or peat moss. Cormels, properly planted and cared for, will grow into flowering bulbs in two seasons.

- **LILY** (*Lilium* sp.): Rivaling the rose for its long-standing history under cultivation, lilies have been grown for ornamental as well as medicinal purposes for thousands of years. Today's lilies come in a wide variety of shapes and sizes, from pristine Easter lilies to orchid-like Madonna lilies to the large and showy oriental varieties. Lilies like sun, but a spot that receives partial shade will not bother them. In fact, it is advisable to shade the lower part of the plant, as lilies like "cold feet."

Perhaps the most irresistible of all flowers, roses have tempted gardeners since the dawn of civilization and, for this reason, merit a few words of their own.

The rose has been under cultivation longer than any other flower. A very famous fancier, Napoleon's Josephine, created

Roses

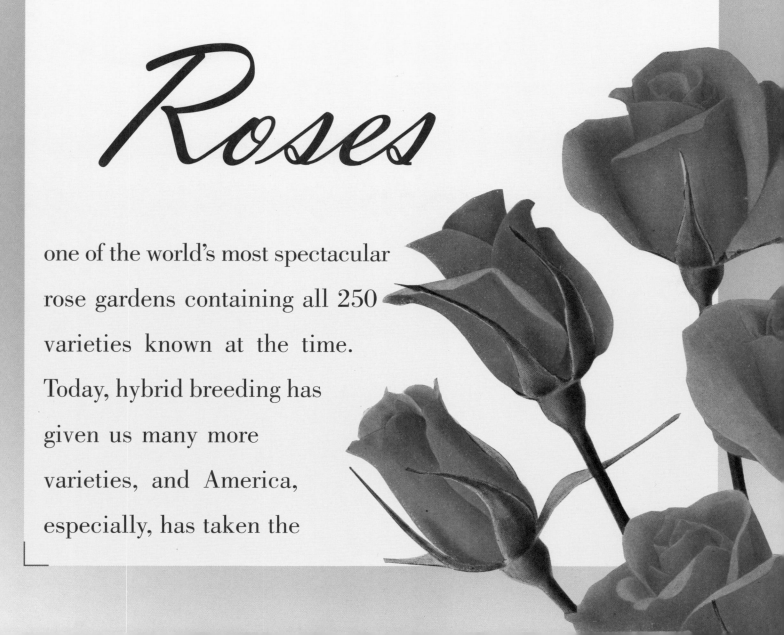

one of the world's most spectacular rose gardens containing all 250 varieties known at the time. Today, hybrid breeding has given us many more varieties, and America, especially, has taken the lead in developing new strains. One of the most popular roses ever, "Peace," was a true collaborative effort—it was smuggled to America from occupied France in 1945.

If you have a craving for this exotic beauty, try your hand—roses aren't as temperamental as people think.

ROSE RULES

1. Buy good bushes.

2. Select a location where you have sun at least half the day and then protect them from the foraging roots of other plants.

3. Plant them properly.

4. Prune them early in the spring.

5. Start weekly cultivation and dusting early in the spring.

6. Protect them in winter.

—*The Complete Book of Garden Magic*, 1935

BUYING PLANTS

Most of the rose plants enjoyed today are hybrids which do not in themselves have the vigor needed for reproduction. To make a healthy hybrid plant, stock is grafted on to hardier foster stock. How well this is done will greatly influence the health, blooming vigor, and life span of the bush. Therefore, it is worthwhile to buy the best plants you can afford from a reliable nursery.

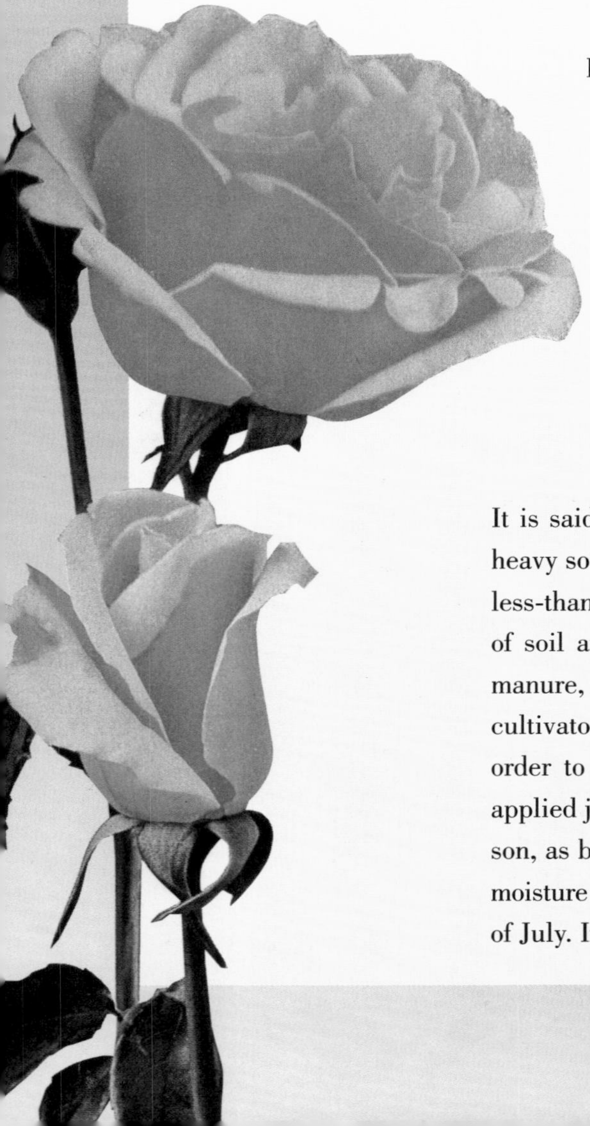

LOCATION OF BUSHES

Roses need an open, sunny location that, ideally, is sheltered by higher ground to the north and west. A southern slope is perfect if you have one. If not, look for a spot that gets sun for the better part of the day and has plenty of open air. Confinement and lack of circulation are invitations to disease and should be avoided. Try not to place bushes close to hedges, walls, and similar obstructions. Also keep them well away from trees and shrubs, whose roots make for stiff competition. If this isn't an option, dig down near the rose bed the full depth of a spade several times a year to cut encroaching roots and keep them from extending into it.

SOIL SPECIFICS

It is said that any type of soil, managed correctly, can accommodate roses. Medium-heavy soil with good drainage and plenty of humus is considered ideal. Compensate for less-than-perfect soil with deep cultivation, taking care that the top six to twelve inches of soil are rich in food—mixed with generous amounts of humus, thoroughly rotted manure, and bone meal. After initial cultivation, working the soil regularly with a hand cultivator is recommended through September, when cultivation should be stopped in order to discourage late-season growth. Applications of chemical fertilizer must be applied judiciously—don't attempt to force plants and never fertilize too late in the season, as both practices will weaken the plant. Some rose growers prefer to conserve soil moisture through dry months by applying a mulch of peat moss or humus at the beginning of July. If you do this, be sure to dust the mulch as well as the plant to prevent fungus.

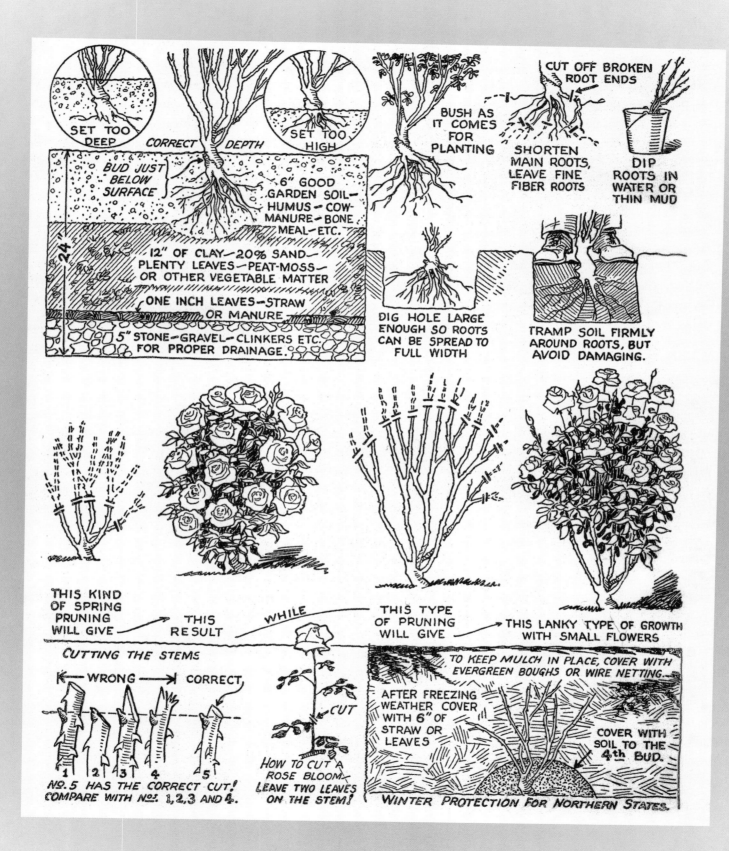

SET TOO DEEP

CORRECT DEPTH

SET TOO HIGH

BUSH AS IT COMES FOR PLANTING

CUT OFF BROKEN ROOT ENDS

SHORTEN MAIN ROOTS, LEAVE FINE FIBER ROOTS

DIP ROOTS IN WATER OR THIN MUD

BUD JUST BELOW SURFACE

6" GOOD GARDEN SOIL—HUMUS—COW MANURE—BONE MEAL—ETC.

12" OF CLAY—20% SAND—PLENTY LEAVES—PEAT-MOSS—OR OTHER VEGETABLE MATTER

ONE INCH LEAVES—STRAW OR MANURE

5" STONE—GRAVEL—CLINKERS ETC. FOR PROPER DRAINAGE.

DIG HOLE LARGE ENOUGH SO ROOTS CAN BE SPREAD TO FULL WIDTH

TRAMP SOIL FIRMLY AROUND ROOTS, BUT AVOID DAMAGING.

THIS KIND OF SPRING PRUNING WILL GIVE → THIS RESULT

WHILE

THIS TYPE OF PRUNING WILL GIVE → THIS LANKY TYPE OF GROWTH WITH SMALL FLOWERS

CUTTING THE STEMS

WRONG — CORRECT

1 2 3 4 5

NO. 5 HAS THE CORRECT CUT! COMPARE WITH NOS. 1, 2, 3 AND 4.

CUT

HOW TO CUT A ROSE BLOOM LEAVE TWO LEAVES ON THE STEM!

TO KEEP MULCH IN PLACE, COVER WITH EVERGREEN BOUGHS OR WIRE NETTING.

AFTER FREEZING WEATHER COVER WITH 6" OF STRAW OR LEAVES

COVER WITH SOIL TO THE 4th BUD.

WINTER PROTECTION FOR NORTHERN STATES.

① SPADE TO A DEPTH OF 1 FT. OR 18 IN.

PLANTING ROSES: TIMING

Roses are best planted in autumn, which allows roots to establish themselves well before blooming begins. If you plant in spring, it should be done as early as the ground can be worked, to give the plant the longest head start possible. Blooming is a stressful time for plants, and the closer you get to this crucial time, the more difficult it will be for the plant to recover.

PLANTING ROSES: HOW-TOS

Most commercially purchased plants come properly pruned and ready for planting. Nevertheless, check the root system and cut off any roots that are damaged or broken. Trim large, thick roots back to six inches from their starting point. Cut back cracked roots as well. They won't heal and will allow disease to enter the plant. You can also cut back what may seem to be "major" roots because it is the small, fibrous roots that take up the most moisture and are the most necessary for the plant's recovery. Of course, if the root system or any other part of the plant appears substantially compromised, return it to the nursery. A good vendor will replace it for you.

One of the "musts" in growing healthy roses is planting them at the proper level. Dig the hole deep enough so that the roots lie naturally, without folding over, and with the tip of the bottom-most root just touching the bottom of the hole. You will want the plant to emerge from the soil just at the point where the main trunk branches into many stems.

After the plant is placed in the hole, fill it with topsoil, packing it down as it is added. When there is enough soil around the roots to protect them, use your feet to tamp the soil.

PRUNING TIPS

Pruning is not done only for aesthetic reasons—to produce a greater number of blooms and keep the plant properly shaped—but also for the health of the plant itself. It encourages new shoots that take the place of exhausted branches and opens the bush to light and air. For this reason, it is a good idea to prune every spring, in most regions during March through mid-April. As a general rule, weaker plants should be pruned more severely than vigorous ones. How you proceed from here depends on what type of rose you have, as tea roses, climbers, ramblers, and other varieties all require differing treatment. For a classic rosebush, cutting the bud stems back below the point where they begin to branch out will produce an attractively round bush with large blooms. It's also best not to have too many of these main stems sprouting from the trunk of the plant—three to five is a good number.

Preparing the bed

Dig in well-rotted horse manure for heavy soils; cow manure for light soils ②

Work in bonemeal, 10 lbs., and muriate or sulphate of potash, 2 lbs., per 100 sq. ft. ③

When buds form, work in tankage, 4 lbs., or cattle manure, 10 lbs., per 100 sq. ft. ④

To prune, make your cut just above a bud that points outward from the plant, cutting on the diagonal so that water will drain off the wound. Make sure your shears are sharp and strong enough for the job, or the resulting tugging and shredding will injure the plant.

Roses, like many other shrubs that are propagated by grafting onto hardier stock, are prone to throw off suckers—fast-growing but unproductive shoots which must be eliminated. Rose suckers can be identified

Rose Gardens, Weequahic Park, Newark, N. J.

because they have seven leaves instead of the characteristic five, as well as by the slick, smooth, overly flexible stem. The best way to deal with these is to cut them off below the soil line to prevent them from robbing the plant of nutrients.

ROSES AND WATER

It is better to conserve moisture already in the soil rather than to try to add more water. However, you will probably have to water in dry weather. Soak the ground so that the roots can absorb the moisture the plant needs. Be sure to soak the plants thoroughly in late autumn before hilling up for the winter.

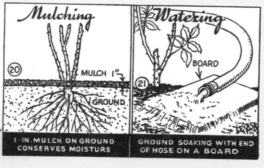

SPRAY OR DUST POWDER ON THE UNDERSIDE OF LEAVES

WINTER HILLING

Rose bushes need protection from drying winter winds. For most plants, hilling will accomplish this nicely. To do this, mound soil around the base of the plant to a height of about eight inches, enough to cover the lowest buds. If you wish to mulch for winter, proceed as for perennials, described on page 78, using only hardwood leaves and creating a structure sufficient to keep the leaves from packing down around the plant.

FIGHTING DISEASE

Roses are particularly susceptible to mildew and fungus. Keeping them pruned helps prevent this, but many rose growers also recommend regular dusting with a good commercial powder (follow the manufacturer's instructions).

Give a boy plenty of grape jam or jelly and at least one feeding habit is fixed for life. I can still remember my first grape pie, although I've had many since. But those grapes of my boyhood seem just a little better . . .

—Fred Gladwin, "Grow Your Own Grapes,"
Better Homes & Gardens, September 1935

Fruit 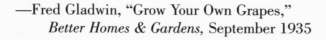 FOR YOUR FAMILY

If you can grow flowers, trees, and shrubs in your yard, there is little reason why you can't grow some type of fruit. In addition to tree fruits such as apples and pears, you may also want to think about growing berries and grapes. One factor to consider when choosing fruits to grow is the region you live in. You are better off to try fruits that do well in your area than exotics that may prove disappointing. However, before you cross anything off your list, consult a local nursery. Today, many hybrids have been adapted for specific climate conditions and you might find exactly what you're looking for.

While fruiting plants need nourishing soil, they are generally less fussy than vegetables, and will also respond better to improved and cultivated ground than many vegetables.

A primary concern is location—exposure is more important to the success of fruit than it is to flowers or even vegetables. Apricots, peaches, and nectarines should not be placed on eastern or southern slopes because the buds may swell early, only to be injured by cold weather in the spring. One way to avoid this is to place these trees on the northern and western sides of buildings or walls. This is not a problem with other tree fruits, berry plants, or grapes.

Space is also a consideration, as fruit will not do well if crowded together. But you needn't despair just because you don't have room for an orchard. You can plant full-sized trees in the yard or take advantage of dwarf varieties. As the illustration at left shows, a twenty-by-twenty-foot space, planted with dwarves, can supply your family with six different types of fruit.

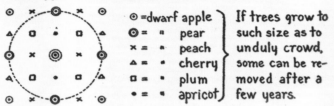

Diagram showing how 25 dwarf trees of six kinds can be grown in the space (20 x 20 ft) required by one standard apple tree — indicated by dotted circles.

⊙ = dwarf apple
◉ = " pear
✕ = " peach
△ = " cherry
□ = " plum
• = " apricot

If trees grow to such size as to unduly crowd, some can be removed after a few years.

FRUIT TREES

In general, fruit trees are handled much like ordinary deciduous trees. There are, however, a few considerations.

- **CHOOSING NURSERY STOCK:** Fruit trees are a substantial investment, and you'll want to take care to pick healthy ones. Insist on a tree with a straight stem that has never been cut or broken. Its branches should be far apart on the trunk, with the three largest pointing in different directions—the ideal arrangement for the development of a well-formed, symmetrical tree. The next best choice is a "whip"—a branchless yearling tree which, by suppressing undesired growth and encouraging well-placed branches, you can guide to symmetrical growth. Never choose a tree with a Y formation. Although this seems the perfect symmetry, and the tree may be healthy and vigorous when you buy it, the tree will split as both branches grow. Another mistake that is often made is buying older, larger trees in the belief that they will yield fruit earlier. They are often still on the market because healthier, more robust trees have already been sold. A younger tree, properly nurtured, will bear fruit earlier than many trees with a "head start."

- **PRUNING AND PLANTING:** Follow the general guidelines as given in "How to Prune Trees and Shrubs," page 56, or consult a local nursery for instructions specific to the tree in question. In most cases, planting in fall or very early spring is recommended because swollen buds are easily injured, and this will slow the tree's recovery. When pruning, be aware that fruit trees are usually cut to achieve one of two shapes, and this shape should be preserved throughout the life of the tree. The "vase" shape is distinguished by three or four main branches, spaced six to ten inches apart, that branch away from the tree at a 45-degree angle. The "central leader" shape has a central, dominant branch that reaches all the way to the top of the tree, with five or six major side branches stemming from it.

- **FEEDING:** The first year after planting, the feeding roots extend only a little way from the base of the tree. Thereafter, roots grow rapidly and forage farther and farther from the base. To feed these roots, you must apply fertilizer in a ring that begins midway between the trunk and the outermost tips of the branches and extends outward twice that distance. If the ground beneath the tree is open and cultivated or is well mulched, fertilize as you would for a vegetable garden. If the ground is planted with grass, double applications are necessary as you are feeding both the fruit plant and the grass.
- **PICKING FRUIT:** Pulling fruit from trees can result in broken, damaged twigs. The proper way to pick tree fruit is to hold the fruit in one hand, the stem in the other, and twist. If the fruit does not come loose readily, it is not yet ripe and should be left on the tree.

APPLES

These are the most widely grown of tree fruits, not only because they are relatively easy to raise but because they are ideal for lawn placement. With the apple, unlike many fruit trees, a well-trimmed cover of grass and clover beneath the tree will suppress trunk and branch growth and stimulate fruit production. While full-sized varieties take up a lot of room, with a leaf spread of as much as forty feet, there are innumerable excellent dwarves that will produce all the fruit you want. Apples prefer deep loam but, in fact, will be fine in less-than-perfect soil so long as it is well managed. Heavy clay soil should be corrected for good drainage, and dry, sandy soil should be well irrigated. If your trees develop small, yellowish leaves and short, spindly shoots, there is insufficient nitrogen in the soil. Apple trees are trimmed to a vase shape, but consult a local nursery before you prune, as different varieties of apple have different pruning times and requirements.

APRICOTS

Native to the Mediterranean, apricot trees require a frost-free climate and sunny location. They prefer well-drained, neutral to slightly alkaline soil and will not flourish in clay or heavy loam. Trees should be watered regularly during their first season and older trees should be watered during dry periods, as they are prone to withering. Fruit forms on both new and old wood, so pruning to keep the vase shape should maintain a balance of both. Fruit spurs (fruit-bearing branches) that have stopped producing should be pruned out. This usually happens after about four years. If the number of developing fruits on the trees is large, the crop should be thinned. When the fruits are pea-sized, thin to one fruit per cluster, then thin again after stones form to about five inches apart.

CHERRIES

Cherries are divided into two classes—sweet and sour. Unfortunately, a dwarf sweet cherry has never been developed, so if you want this type of tree, you will need a space about thirty feet in diameter. Sour cherries do come in dwarf varieties and are far easier to grow, doing well in almost any condition. Sweet cherries require light to medium loam, but sour cherries will tolerate even poor soil as long as it is not waterlogged. All cherries, whether sweet or sour, dislike heavy, poorly drained soil. Because sweet cherries bear fruit on older wood, minimal pruning—just enough to keep the tree open and well proportioned—is required. Sour cherries bear fruit on the previous season's shoots, and this makes pruning a more complex matter, as the gardener must select which buds to allow to develop and which to pinch back. Trees of both types are generally pruned to a central leader shape. Birds are the biggest challenge to your harvest and will decimate a crop unless the trees are covered with protective netting.

PEACHES

If you live in a temperate climate with abundant sunshine, you owe it to yourself to enjoy the sumptuous delight of tree-ripened peaches: nothing compares with a home-grown peach's taste and texture. Peach trees do best in light

soil that is not too rich. Growing in sod should be avoided—it invites attacks from borers—so remove the grass from the area around the peach tree trunk. Fruit forms on the previous season's growth, so prune shoots in a vase shape to give you a desirable amount of new growth.

PEARS

Although some people consider apples the rugged, grow-anywhere fruit tree, pears are nearly as easy to raise. Pears can withstand poor drainage better than apples, but are less able to tolerate drought. They come in both standard and dwarf varieties, and do best in deep, rich loam that is slightly acidic. Alkaline soil should be avoided as pears are prone to iron deficiency. Trees should be pruned sparingly until they begin to bear fruit. Thereafter, prune central leader style in a pyramid shape, but do not over-prune as this will promote suckers.

PLUMS

More than other tree fruits, different strains of plum require different growing conditions, so buying thriving plants at a nursery near your home is an especially good idea. Almost all plums need good drainage, but European varieties prefer heavy loam while American and Japanese types do best in soil that is sandy or even gravelly. One of the biggest problems with plum trees is that too many fruits will form. This is dangerous because the tree's wood is naturally brittle, and breaks easily when over-burdened. Thinning fruits early on helps, but providing support for laden branches (by means of a wide, notched stake on which the branch can rest) may be necessary. Heavy pruning in a vase shape will help limit the crop, and some experts advise pruning back one third to one half of new growth.

BERRIES

Berries are surprisingly easy to grow. With the exception of the strawberry, which is not a true fruit, most berries are either bush or cane fruits. The chief difference between these types is that cane fruits, like vines, are not self-supporting, and must have a fence or wires which they can be trained to. Bush fruits do not need support, and can generally grow in any location that receives sunlight most of the day.

BLACKBERRIES

As with all cane fruits, blackberries require good drainage, and the spot you pick should meet this requirement. If the ground remains wet and soggy after a heavy rain, pick a different location or cultivate deeper than you ordinarily would, digging down a foot or more, to correct the problem. Blackberries should be planted in the fall, in a location that affords some shelter from strong winds. They are rampant growers and must be controlled to achieve well-developed, full-sized berries. The best way to do this is to reduce the number of canes each spring so there is only one every ten feet; pull up all the others. Remaining canes can either be pinched off at the tips when they are about thirty inches tall (to encourage branching), or fastened to a support wire when they reach a height of thirty-six inches. Blackberry stems are biennial, growing one season and bearing fruit the next. Cut stems close to the ground as soon as they are done bearing fruit. In the spring, stems on canes that were pinched back the previous season should be cut back to a height of about eighteen inches. Canes that weren't pinched should be cut back to about forty inches.

The biggest problem with blackberries is suppressing the prolific suckers. These nonbearing branches will form a dense and thorny thicket unless you eliminate them as soon as they appear. This must be done by pulling them up—cutting them off will only cause more suckers to grow from the stumps.

RASPBERRIES

Raspberries are also cane fruits and resemble blackberries in their soil preferences. However, they come in a greater number of varieties than do blackberries, having either red, black, or golden fruit and being propagated from roots and root cuttings as well as by rooting branch tips. Whether you should plant in the spring or fall depends upon the variety in question, so consult a local nursery. Like blackberries, raspberry stems are biennial, bearing fruit in their second season, and should be trained and managed as for blackberries. There is one exception—red varieties should not be pinched.

BLUEBERRIES

Blueberries are bush fruits that require the least care of all the berries. They prefer an acidic soil of sandy loam to which peat moss or humus is added. The area around the plant should be kept open and cultivated but, since the root system is shallow, you need only cultivate to a depth of about two inches. Plants should be kept well watered throughout the summer, but fertilization is not necessary until the beginning of the third year. Branches that have ceased bearing should be cut back to ground level during the dormant season, and branches that rub against each other should also be pruned back.

STRAWBERRY CULTIVATION
— PLANTING —

WRONG / RIGHT

ROOTS NOT COVERED
PLANTED TOO DEEP
ROOTS TOO CROWDED

TRIM ROOTS BEFORE PLANTING
CROWN LEVEL WITH GROUND
ROOTS COMPLETELY COVERED AND UNCROWDED

WHEN PLANTING, ADD A TEASPOONFUL OF CARBON DISULPHIDE TO EACH PLANT AT ROOTS TO PREVENT GRUBS

ROWS 3 FT. APART
PLANTS 1 FT. APART.

W. P. BAKER.

After planting apply a mixture of 5 lbs. superphosphate, 5 lbs. potash, and 1 lb. dried blood. Rake into soil around plants and between rows 1 pound to 50 square feet.

STRAWBERRIES

Technically speaking, the strawberry is not a fruit but a vegetable. While needing a bit more care than the other berries described above, it is nevertheless easy to grow and well worth the labor. The strawberry is grown in rows in a dirt plot. All strawberry varieties need well-drained soil, and should not be planted where tomatoes, potatoes, peppers, or bulbs have been grown. Plants should be set out in the spring, with about eighteen to twenty-four inches between plants. The depth at which strawberries are planted is important. The crown (plant above the roots) should emerge exactly at the soil line, but the plant should not be so high that the roots are exposed to air.

The key to growing strawberries is patience. Do not expect to get fruit the first year. Instead, pinch off the first spring's flowers. This will build up the plants and reward you in seasons to come.

In early summer, plants will send out runners (vine-like shoots) which, if allowed to, will take root and form new plants. How you deal with these runners depends on the type of strawberry patch you want and, ultimately, upon the type of fruit you prefer. If you let the runners root at random, you will have matted rows, with plants that produce a

great number of small-sized berries. If you cut back the runners and do not allow them to root at all, the original plants will develop into hills, which produce the largest and finest berries but in smaller numbers. You can also let only some new plants form, which allows you to control the size of your patch and maintain plants in rows. If you wish to do this, remember that the first leaf cluster on a runner will produce the best plant.

One thing to consider when deciding whether or not to let runners grow is to remember that strawberry plants need regular cultivation of the soil, both to keep the soil moist and to eliminate weeds. This is a lot of work, and maintaining plants in hills or neat rows will allow you to use a hoe for this work. If the rows become matted with random-growing plants, this work needs to be done on hands and knees.

Strawberry plants have shallow roots and need winter protection against heaving—or being pulled up—as the soil freezes and thaws. After the ground has completely frozen, apply a mulch of straw, shredded corn stalks, or other weed-free material. The plants should be uncovered as soon as they begin to grow in the spring. Instead of removing the mulch, rake it between the rows to conserve moisture in the soil.

GRAPES

Of all the fruits, probably the grape appeals to the home gardener in greater degree than any other.
It responds so readily to good care, and the various operations are literally within an arm's reach, as it were.
It's comparatively easy to prune a grape vine, or spray; and the harvesting is simple, compared to picking
tree fruits. Then the joy of lifting the pendant grape canes in the fall and viewing the well-filled luscious clusters
where none seem to have been is quite like dipping into the proverbial grab bag and drawing forth a prize.
Growing grapes thus appeases the inner self as well as the physical satisfaction of taste.

—Fred Gladwin, "Grow Your Own Grapes,"
Better Homes & Gardens, September 1935

Not much has changed since Fred Gladwin began growing grapes in 1915, except that far too many people have come to think of grapes as a California-only crop. Nothing could be further from the truth. Gladwin conducted his thriving business from upstate New York, a region not known for sunny skies or mild winters. Another grape myth is that you need elaborate trellises to accommodate the plants. Gladwin explains that he got into the business by accident when his father used them to beautify some weathered outbuildings. The grape canes, fastened to the clapboards with strips of sheepskin, prospered so well that soon neighbors, and eventually nurseries, were asking to buy plants. Here, then, are one expert's secrets for growing healthy, fruit-bearing vines. Note that planting is done in the spring and that, for the first season, no trellis is necessary.

- **CHOOSING PLANTS:** Select varieties that suit your growing season. Plant more than one variety, including both early- and late-ripening vines, as well as "eating" grapes and those better suited for jams and jellies.

- **PREPARING TO PLANT:** Allot a space of about eight feet on all sides. Holes should be dug somewhat larger and deeper than the roots seem to require. Do not add manure or fertilizer to the hole. However, well-rotted manure or a few handfuls of nitrate of soda can be spread in a three-foot radius from the center of the hole.

- **IMMEDIATELY BEFORE PLANTING:** Use shears or a sharp knife to cut all broken or bruised roots. Clip all roots to twelve to fifteen inches from the base of the trunk.

- **PLANTING:** Place a two-to-three-inch layer of topsoil in the freshly dug hole and pack it down. Plant the vine so that the roots are evenly distributed over the soil. Cover with a layer of topsoil and tamp it down. Repeat this until the hole is filled, ending with a slight mound to compensate for settling.

- **AFTER PLANTING:** Cut away all but one of the previous year's growths from the old wood where it projects above the ground. Cut the growth you have selected to keep back and make a spur of two or three buds. Keep weeds cut to a low level until late summer. If the plants require support, stake them as you would any other plant.

- **THE FOLLOWING SPRING:** Erect a trellis using iron posts set twenty-four feet apart and strung with No. 10 wire. Canes should be fastened to the trellis with strong materials that will not cut or injure the vine, such as twine or raffia. Fastenings should be made immediately below the outermost bud.

- **YEARS ONE THROUGH FOUR:** Pick all fruit before ripening during the first and second years. The third year, allow a partial crop, letting half the fruit ripen on the vine. In the fourth year, a full crop can be matured and harvested.

Q.: How to care for a two-year-old Concord grape vine that has made fine growth this past summer. I would like to protect it from the extreme cold of our Maine winter. Should it be pruned very much and what about a mulch at the base?

A.: If the vine is on a trellis, it ought to come through the winter safely, providing you give it a mulch of protective material. Salt hay, peat moss, leaves held down with burlap or evergreen branches, or other loose material will be satisfactory. Don't use mulch until hard freezing has set in. Heap it up about 6" around the main growing stem or stems. Most people do the necessary grape pruning in late winter (February or March) when a favorable day for such work comes along.

—The Home Garden, February 1944

- **PRUNING:** To get a full, well-ripened harvest, it is essential to reduce the number of buds each season. This pruning should only be done during the dormant period. Vigorous vines can bear up to forty buds, but less vigorous vines should be cut back to twenty or even less. Here's an additional hint: Just before the blossom clusters open, snip off one-fourth to one-third of the clusters with ordinary kitchen shears, eliminating any that seem small or poorly formed.

- **FERTILIZATION:** A good commercial plant food or a few handfuls of nitrate of soda may be used to enrich soil. Cut back weeds until late summer, to avoid competition. If you have too much leaf and cane growth and too little fruit, withhold nitrogen-rich food for a year or two.

TOMATO

PONDEROSA

5¢

There is a real beauty in ordered rows and vari-colored green as well as in vegetables themselves. Take, for example, rosette lettuce, gray-headed cabbages, creamy-white cauliflowers, red-stemmed beet tops, filmy-leaved carrots,

THE *Vegetable* GARDEN

curly kale, green-blossomed broccoli, shiny-leaved peppers with their green and red fruits, and great-leaved corn with tasseled ears. Surely no one can miss their decorative quality.

—Better Homes & Gardens,
March 1933

GARDEN
V
FOR
VICTORY

Vegetable gardens can be beautiful but, more than that, they are deeply satisfying. Who in their heart doesn't believe that a carrot grown in one's own backyard tastes better than one that comes from the store? Yet many people think growing vegetables requires a lot of time and space. Neither of these are true, if you adopt some time-tested strategies.

BEST GARDEN SITES

If you have a choice of locations, pick a spot that gets full exposure to the sun and can accommodate a plot that is longer from north to south than from east to west. This will make for the most even distribution of sunlight along the rows. The plot should also be well-drained—vegetables do not grow well in poorly drained soil and good drainage will help the ground warm up in the spring. If the plot is on slightly raised ground, so much the better, as this too favors spring warming.

THE PERFECT SOIL MIX

The best soil for vegetables is loam, made up of sand, clay, and humus. If your soil is not as rich as desired, build it by adding humus-forming materials such as compost and leaf mold. Horse manure is especially good for this purpose, and worth purchasing. If your plot contains too much clay or has been in sod for several years, begin the autumn by spreading a layer of well-rotted manure, then digging it under, and leaving the ground rough through the winter. Lighter soil can be conditioned in early spring, as soon as the soil no longer appears wet. Once every several years, practice double digging or trenching as described in "Soil: The Key Ingredient," page 32.

MAKING THE MOST OF TIME AND SPACE

Before you begin drawing a plan for your vegetable plot, you'll want to decide which crops to grow. A word of advice: don't grow any vegetable you don't like, simply because it's easy to raise. However, your likes and dislikes aren't the only considerations either. Space and economy also matter. As you make your list of desired crops, pay attention to these important factors:

- **VEGETABLES THAT YIELD MOST** (in proportion to the space they occupy and the time required to grow them): beets, broccoli, cabbage, carrots, chard, Chinese cabbage, cress, dwarf beans, lettuce, mustard, New Zealand spinach, onions (from sets), pole beans, radishes, rutabagas, spinach, tomatoes, turnips.

- **VEGETABLES REQUIRING LEAST SPACE:** beets, carrots, chard, Chinese cabbage, cress, dwarf beans, leaf lettuce, leeks, mustard, onions, pole beans, radishes, rutabagas, tampala, tomatoes, turnips.

- **VEGETABLES REQUIRING CONSIDERABLE SPACE** (those marked "*" should be provided with three feet or more of space between rows): broccoli, cabbage, cauliflower, corn*, cucumbers*, eggplants, melons*, New Zealand spinach, parsnips, peas, peppers, potatoes*, squash*, sweet potatoes*.

- **VEGETABLES THAT GROW DURING A SHORT SEASON:** beets, bush beans, early cabbage, carrots, kohlrabi, lettuce, mustard, onions (from sets), peas, radishes, spinach, turnips.

- **VEGETABLES THAT ARE DIFFICULT TO GROW IN MANY REGIONS:** cauliflower, celery, Chinese cabbage, cucumber, onions (from seed), peas, potatoes, pumpkins, spinach, squash (winter varieties).

—The Home Garden, February 1944

MAKING THE MOST OF YOUR VEGETABLE GARDEN

Vegetable gardeners are second only to baseball managers in their ability to strategize, and there are several ways you can expand the number of crops your garden can accommodate. As you continue developing your crop list, consider these time-honored practices:

- **SUCCESSION CROPPING:** Crops that grow and mature quickly are replaced by another crop after they are harvested. For example, spinach or early peas could be followed by bush beans which, in turn, could be followed by turnips or winter radish.

- **COMPANION CROPPING:** Two or three crops that must be sown at the same time but mature at different times are planted as alternate rows, or as alternate plants in the same row. This maximizes space, as rows and plants can be set closer together without fear of crowding. Likely combinations are spinach alternated with beets or lettuce alternated with cabbage in even-numbered rows and odd-numbered rows planted entirely with radishes. It's also possible to sow quickly maturing crops among perennial vegetables—spinach and lettuce are common pairings with the perennial asparagus, and will be finished before the perennial begins to mature.

- **PARTNERSHIP CROPPING:** In some cases, crops are so compatible they can be planted together regardless of their maturation dates. For example, corn is no threat to pumpkins, winter squash, melons, or cucumbers—ground-running vines that can grow without a lot of sunlight.

Before you can make a plan that takes advantage of these strategies, you must know how much time each vegetable needs to reach maturity. Consult the following At-a-Glance Crop Guide and the more detailed Planting Chart.

AT-A-GLANCE CROP GUIDE

- **EARLY SPRING TO LATE SPRING:** cress, early lettuce, forced radish, lamb's lettuce, mustard, onion sets, spinach.
- **EARLY SPRING TO MIDSUMMER OR EARLY FALL:** beet, carrot, early celery, early radish, kohlrabi, long-rooted radish, onion, pea, turnip.
- **ALL SEASON (EARLY SPRING TO LATE FALL):** celeriac, chard, chicory, leek, parsley, parsnip, salsify.
- **LATE SPRING TO EARLY FALL:** bean, eggplant, gherkin, husk tomato (ground cherry), okra, pepper, pumpkin, sweet potato, squash, tomato.
- **MIDSUMMER TO LATE FALL:** beet, broccoli, Brussels sprout, carrot, cauliflower, endive, late cabbage, late celery, kale, kohlrabi, rutabaga, turnip.
- **LATE SUMMER TO LATE FALL:** cress, forcing radish, lettuce, mustard, onion sets, round-seeded pea, spinach, winter radish.

—*The Complete Book of Garden Magic*, 1935

PLANTING CHART

Exactly when you can begin seeds indoors or outdoors depends on the climate you live in, and the guidelines you are given below are both broad and general. If you begin plants indoors, you will need to figure out when you can expect to move them and plan backwards to determine when to start your seeds. When it's time to move plants outdoors, you want your seedlings to be well-established, but not so large that they have become cramped and crowded. Another climate-dependent variable is what it means to "set out" your plants. In warmer regions, this can mean transplanting directly into the soil. But in colder regions, where days may be warm but temperatures dip quite low at night, it may mean setting pots out during the day but bringing them to shelter at night. The advantage of acclimatizing plants in this way, instead of simply leaving them inside until it's good and warm out, is that the plants become hardier and, ultimately, more productive.

Name	Seed Required for 50 ft. Row	Time to Start Seed in Hotbed or Greenhouse	Time to Transplant Seedlings to Garden	Time to Sow Seed in Open Garden	Rows Apart (in feet)	Plants Apart in Row (In.)	Depth of Planting (In.)	Degree of Hardiness
Beans—(Bush)	½ pt.	....	....	April–May	1½–2	4	1½	Tender
Beans—(Pole)	½ pt.	....	....	May	4	36	1½–2	Very tender
Beans—Lima (Bush)	½ pt.	....	....	May 15	1½–2	4	1½–2	Very tender
Beans—Lima (Pole)	½ pt.	....	....	May 15	4	36	1½–2	Very tender
Beets (Early)	1 oz.	February	April	April	1½	4	½	Hardy
Beets (Late)	1 oz.	....	....	June–July	1½	4	½	Hardy
Carrot (Early)	½ oz.	....	....	April	1½–2	2–4	½	Hardy
Carrot (Late)	½ oz.	....	....	July–August	1½–2	2–4	½	Hardy
Chard (Swiss)	1 oz.	....	....	April	1½	6–8	¾	Hardy
Cress	....	....	....	April–May	1–1½	2–3	½	Hardy
Dill	....	....	....	April	1½	4–6	½	
Endive	¼ oz.	....	....	April	1½–1½	8–12	½	Tender
Lettuce	¼ oz.	Feb.–Mar.	April 15	April	1½–2	8–12	¼	Hardy
Mustard	1 oz.	....	....	April	1½–2	8–10	½	Tender
Onions (Sets)	1 qt.	....	....	April	1–1½	2–3	½	Hardy
Peas	1 lb.	....	....	April	6–8 Double Row	6	2	Hardy
Potato (Early)	4–5 lbs.	....	....	April	3	6–8	4	Hardy
Radish	½ oz.	Feb.–Mar.	....	April	1½–2	1–3	½	Hardy

Name	Seed Required for 50 ft. Row	Time to Start Seed in Hotbed or Greenhouse	Time to Transplant Seedlings to Garden	Time to Sow Seed in Open Garden	Rows Apart (in feet)	Plants Apart in Row (In.)	Depth of Planting (In.)	Degree of Hardiness
Artichoke, Jerusalem	4–5 lbs.	....	....	April	3–4	24–36	4	Tender
Broccoli	¼ oz.	....	....	April–May	2½–3	24	½–1	Hardy
Brussels Sprouts	¼ oz.	March	May	April	2½–3	18–24	½	Hardy
Cabbage (Early)	¼ oz.	Feb.–Mar.	May	April	2–3	24	½	Hardy
Cabbage (Late)	¼ oz.	....	....	May	2–3	24	½	Hardy
Cabbage (Savoy)	¼ oz.	....	....	May	2–3	24	½	Hardy
Cardoon	¼ oz.	Feb.–Mar.	May	....	3	18	½	Tender
Cauliflower	¼ oz.	Jan.–Feb.	May	....	2–3	15	½	Tender
Celeriac	¼ oz.	March	May	April	2	9	¼	Hardy
Celery	¼ oz.	Feb.–Mar.	May–June	April	2–3	6–8	¼	Hardy
Chicory	....	....	....	April	1–2	10–12	½	Hardy
Collards	¼ oz.	Feb.–Mar.	....	May	3	24–36	½	Hardy
Corn (Sweet)	½ pt.	....	....	May	3	24–36	1	Tender
Cucumbers	½ oz.	....	....	May–June	3–4	36–48	1	Tender
Egg Plant	¼ oz.	Feb.–Mar.	May	....	3	24	½	Tender
Kale (see Broccoli)	above)	....	....	....	....	....	....	....
Kohl Rabi	¼ oz.	....	....	April	1½–2	8–12	½	Hardy
Leek	½ oz.	....	....	April	1¼–2	4–6	½	Very Hardy
Muskmelon	¼ oz.	....	....	May	3–4	36–48	1	Tender
New Zealand Spinach	¼ oz.	....	....	May	3	12–18	½	Hardy
Okra	1 oz.	April	June	May	3	12	½	Tender
Parsley	½ oz.	....	....	April	1	4–6	½	Hardy
Parsnip	¼ oz.	....	....	April	1½	4	½	Hardy
Peppers	¼ oz.	Feb.–Mar.	May	May	2	24	½	Tender
Potato (Late)	4–5 lbs.	....	....	May–June	3	6–8	4	Hardy
Pumpkins	½ oz.	....	....	May	4–5	36–48	1	Tender
Rutabaga	½ oz.	....	....	April	2½	8–12	½	Hardy
Salsify	1 oz.	....	....	April	1½	4	½	Hardy
Spinach	1 oz.	....	....	April	1–1½	6	½	Hardy
Squash	½ oz.	....	....	May–June	4–5	48–60	½	Very Tender
Sweet Potato	50 roots	March	May–June	....	3–5	14	3–4	Tender
Tomato	¼ oz.	March	May	....	2½–3	30–36	½	Tender
Turnip	½ oz.	....	....	April	1½–2	3–4	½	Hardy
Watermelon	1 oz.	....	....	May	8–10	80–90	1	Tender

Name	Seed Required for 50 ft. Row	Time to Start Seed in Hotbed or Greenhouse	Time to Transplant Seedlings to Garden	Time to Sow Seed in Open Garden	Rows Apart (in feet)	Plants Apart in Row (In.)	Depth of Planting (In.)	Degree of Hardiness
Artichoke, Globe	½ oz.	Feb.–Mar.	May	....	3–4	24	½	Hardy
Asparagus	40 plants	....	....	April	1½–3	14	4–5	Hardy
Dandelion	½ oz.	....	....	May	1½	8–10	½	Hardy
Horseradish	50 roots	....	....	April	2	8–12	2	Hardy
Rhubarb	25 roots	....	....	May	2½–3	24	¾	Hardy

PLANTING CHART

PLANTS

Successive Planting (Days Apart)	Days to Mature	Important Suggestions
14 days to July Season	60	Early plantings can be followed by Fall vegetables.
	60	Longer bearing than above. Use poles 6–8 ft. long, plant 6 seeds per pole and later thin to [three.
10 days to July Season	60	Cultivate as for Bush Snap Beans above.
	60	Plant and thin as for Pole Snap Beans above.
14 days	40–70	Late plantings for Winter use should use turnip varieties.
. . . .	90	Before freezing, dig and store in cellar or pit.
14 days	100	Hoe deeply and frequently—keep clean of weeds.
	120	Give plenty of water and keep soil well cultivated.
20–30	60–70	Can replant until September for Fall and Winter use.
14 days to Sept.	35	Easily grown in Winter in greenhouse, hotbed or window box.
Fall use in June	100–120	Tie outer leaves over center bud when 6 to 8 inches long.
August	70–90	Fertilize heavily—plant on rich soil and supply abundant moisture.
7 days	30–40	Can be grown in window boxes in Spring.
14 days	50–60	Till top soil frequently and keep free of weeds.
7–14 days	60	Do best in cool weather, so plant as early as possible.
June for Fall	90	Apply fertilizer between rows several times during season.
7–10 days	30	For Fall use long, white varieties.

PLANTS

Successive Planting (Days Apart)	Days to Mature	Important Suggestions
. . . .	5–6 mos.	Plant 3 or 4 small tubers in a hill.
. . . .	4–5 mos.	Winter crop may be started in May.
14 days	5–6 mos.	When small sprouts begin to appear—Cut large leaves off to favor sprouts.
. . . .	4–5 mos.	
. . . .	4–5 mos.	Fertilize and cultivate freely—Hill up slightly as growth progresses.
. . . .	4–5 mos.	
. . . .	5–6 mos.	Leaves bunched for blanching in early Fall.
. . . .	4–5 mos.	Never allow plants to become checked in growth.
. . . .	5–6 mos.	Blanching not required—Roots remain in ground until wanted.
. . . .	5–6 mos.	See "Vegetable Guide" for information on blanching.
. . . .	6–7 mos.	Then raised and transplanted in trench and covered with manure—After 4 to 5 weeks ready [for use.
June	3–4 mos.	Stands hot weather better than cabbage or kale. Grown widely in Southern States.
10 days to June	2–3 mos.	Deep soil and frequent cultivation makes best crop.
. . . .	2–3 mos.	Plant in low hills for perfect drainage while young.
. . . .	4–5 mos.	Grow best in well drained, warm soil.
. . . .	2½–3 mos.	Quite hardy and does well where cauliflower cannot be grown.
. . . .	3–4 mos.	Plant in open furrow 5 or 6 inches deep—Draw in earth as plants grow to level of garden.
. . . .	3–4 mos.	Plant in hills, 10 to 12 seed, thin to 4 plants.
. . . .	3–4 mos.	Soak seed 2 hours in hot water.
June	3 mos.	Requires frequent cultivation until plants cover the ground.
May–June	3–4 mos.	Seed germinate very slowly—mark rows with radish seeds.
. . . .	4–5 mos.	Better flavored if subjected to early frosts.
. . . .	4–5 mos.	Top dress soil between rows when plants 6 inches high.
. . . .	4–5 mos.	Dig before hard freezing.
. . . .	4–5 mos.	Plant on hills and cultivate as for cucumbers.
. . . .	4–5 mos.	Pull roots before freezing, cut off tops and store in cellar.
. . . .	4–5 mos.	Dig roots in Fall or Winter as required.
. . . .	3 mos.	Apply nitrate of soda between rows to stimulate growth.
. . . .	2–4 mos.	Winter squash may be planted later and stored for use in moderately warm, dry place.
. . . .	5–6 mos.	Dig when vines have been killed by frost.
June	4–5 mos.	Protect from frost when first set out in garden.
June–July	2–3 mos.	Crowding or weeds make poorly flavored roots.
. . . .	4–5 mos.	Top dress with fertilizer high in nitrogen and potash.

PLANTS

Successive Planting (Days Apart)	Days to Mature	Important Suggestions
. . . .	Aug.–Sept.	If crowns get too large after two or three years—divide and reset.
. . . .	May–June	In northern states mulch asparagus to prevent heaving of the roots during winter.
. . . .	Sept. (1st. yr.)	Blanch by covering with straw or leaves.
. . . .		Tends to become rank weed—cultivate closely and root out volunteers.
. . . .	2nd Spring	Keep blossom stalks cut back—flowers and seed exhaust plant.

—The Complete Book of Garden Magic, 1935

VEGETABLES: MAKING A PLAN

Once a crop list is developed, it's time to plan the garden layout. The easiest way to do this is on a piece of graph paper scaled to the dimensions of your plot. It may also be helpful to cut individual strips of paper to represent rows of different crops you want to grow, labeling each strip with the name of the crop (or crops) planned for that row, the space required between rows, and the number of days to maturity. This way, you can arrange and rearrange your plot, without having to redraw it each time. Here are some other things to consider as you create your plan:

Laying out a garden—Sheet of paper on drawing or bread board—Use loose strips of paper to represent different crops.

Always firm soil well after sowing seed with board or by treading—especially in light soils.

Tillage is essential—use wheel hoe with different interchangeable parts—or any of various kinds of hoes

How to dig light and heavy soils

Dig deep for root crops.   Simple way to store celery

Thin out seedlings to permit good growth. — Thinned out plants can be cooked and eaten too.

For small gardens hand weeding is practical— Here are types of hand weeders.

- Place tall crops such as sweet corn, pole beans, and staked tomatoes at the ends of the garden or on the north side, where they will not block the sun for low-growing crops.
- Plant crops in groups according to their growing time. Divide your garden to accommodate:
1. Succession planting, in which an area is planted first with quickly maturing plants, then planted with a second fast-growing crop after the first is harvested.
2. Slow-growing crops that will need all season to mature.
3. Companion crops, which occupy the ground at the same time but develop and mature at different times.
- Practice crop rotation. If possible, shift crops (or groups of crops) to different sections of your garden plot from year to year. This helps keep soil from becoming depleted and makes it harder for pests and plant diseases to become established.
- Make a permanent, weatherproof copy of your plan as a reminder of where you want to plant something. Having a copy of your plan on durable cardboard, in waterproof pen or pencil, and annotated with crop names and with distances between rows, will save a lot of running back and forth.

GETTING YOUR GARDEN GROWING

*We start our garden early—very early. There always seems to be a
week or two of nice warm weather around the first of March which makes it just right
for a bed of early onions, radishes, lettuce and those potatoes which some people
plant on St. Patrick's day regardless of the weather. If it snows on your early beds of
vegetables or turns cold, don't worry about them. They will be all ready
to pop through the ground when the next warm sunshiny days come. We are really
justified in eating our onions and radishes when some of our neighbors are
just getting in the mood to make a garden.*

—*The Modern Family Garden Book*, 1941

For most gardeners, enthusiasm for the summer garden rises as the winter months depart. That's why it's good to have your soil prepared and ready to go, and to have included at least a few "early" crops in your plan. Here are some tips to take you through the garden season:

- **DIG AND RAKE:** Before sowing seeds or setting out plants, always dig and rake the soil anew, even if it was recently cultivated. Only dig the soil that you will actually plant that day.
- **SOW SEEDS:** As a rule of thumb, spring seeds should be planted three to four times as deep as their diameter, and firmed lightly with the head of a rake. Summer-sown seeds should be planted deeper and pressed into the ground more firmly. Larger seeds, such as peas and beans, do best if you first tamp the row firmly, then cover them with loosely raked soil. You will save yourself a good deal of trouble if you lightly rake the entire bed in the direction of the rows with a steel rake soon after sowing, then repeat the process with a bamboo or metal broom rake within a week. This will kill thousands of tiny weedlings and break the soil crust which lets your crop sprout.

A BALL OF TWINE

*When planting in rows, remember
that nothing speeds up weeding and
general cultivation like straight lines of plants.
This applies especially when a wheel hoe is used.
A few extra minutes with a ball of twine now
will subtract many minutes and a good deal
of backache later.*

—*Better Homes & Gardens*, March 1933

113

A convenient way to make drills and sow seed in good straight rows is to use a board, pressing the narrow edge down into the soil to the desired depth.

—*House and Garden,* April 1912

- **LABEL:** It is easy to forget what is planted where. That's why it's always a good idea to label your rows.
- **THIN:** When plants have developed two or three pairs of true leaves, thin them as recommended on the seed packet. Thinned plants can be discarded or transplanted to make new rows or to fill in gaps. In some cases, such as leaf lettuce and early beets, the thinned plants can actually be eaten!
- **SETTING OUT PLANTS:** As described previously, some plants must be started indoors and only moved outdoors when they become thriving seedlings. After the plants have been set out, rake as described for sown seeds, being careful

not to injure the plants or their roots. Thereafter, cultivate between plants and rows frequently to maintain a dirt mulch.

- **EARLY CARE:** Until plants are big enough for their foliage to shade the ground, hoe the soil after every rain, as soon as a crust has formed and dried.
- **WATERING:** Few plants benefit from a mere sprinkling of water. This is true for vegetables as well. True watering should penetrate a foot down into the soil, and should be followed by cultivation to prevent clumping. In the long run, it will take less water to give your crops a good, occasional soaking than a daily sprinkling that will do them no good at all.
- **WEED:** Perhaps the most disliked of garden chores, weeding is also among the most necessary. Not only does it prevent moisture and nourishment from leeching out of the soil, it is important for keeping pests at bay.
- **HARVEST:** After the plant is harvested of its food and will yield no more, dig it up, if it is an annual, and take it to the compost pile or rubbish heap. Leaving it in the ground wastes plant food and water, and provides a home for many pests. Prepare the vacant soil and plant it with another crop, either a vegetable or a suitable ground cover, to prevent it from becoming overrun with weeds.
- **STORAGE:** You can make late fall crops last longer if you learn to store them correctly. Such crops fall into four categories:
1. Crops that can be left in the ground over the winter, such as Jerusalem artichoke and parsnip.
2. Crops that must be kept cold, dark, but not too dry after they are dug, such as beet, Brussels sprout, cabbage, carrot, cauliflower, celery, eggplant, leek, pepper, potato, rutabaga, and winter radish. (These can be "planted" in boxes of granulated peat moss and kept in a garage.)
3. Crops that must be kept cold and dry, including onion and garlic.
4. Crops that must be kept warm and dry, including pumpkin and winter squash.

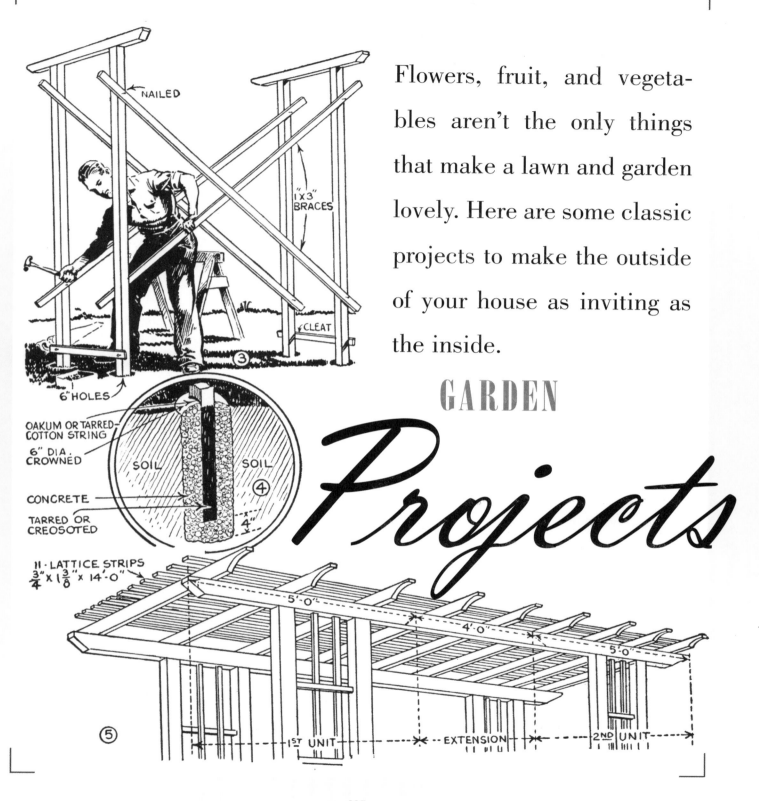

Flowers, fruit, and vegetables aren't the only things that make a lawn and garden lovely. Here are some classic projects to make the outside of your house as inviting as the inside.

SPICE UP YOUR GARDEN

If you like the idea of doing things the old fashioned way, try planting an herb garden. During the Middle Ages, when herbs served both medicinal and culinary purposes, these gardens enjoyed their first surge of widespread popularity. They were laid out along formal lines, subdivided into geometrically patterned beds, and adorned with winding paths and decorative borders. Monastery gardens often featured a soothing "Mint Pool" where one could sit, reflect, and refresh the spirit. So if your spirit—or your cooking—need revitalization, try herbs.

TIPS FOR STARTING AN HERB GARDEN

- **SELECT THE RIGHT LOCATION:** When it comes to deciding where to put your plot, remember that drainage is more important than any other factor. Herbs will not grow in wet, poorly drained soil. The second most important factor is light—with few exceptions, herbs require full sunlight to do well.

- **CHOOSE YOUR HERBS:** There are so many herbs to choose from you may feel a bit overwhelmed. Don't be—just think of herbs you like and will actually enjoying using. A good mix for beginners might include rosemary, sage, basil, dill, mint, marjoram, tarragon, thyme, oregano, chives, and parsley.

- **MAKE A PLAN:** As with flowers, position tall herbs, such as dill, so they will not shade their shorter companions. It will also make for easier maintenance to keep annual herbs separate from perennial ones. Common annuals include anise, basil, chervil, coriander, dill, and summer savory. Perennials include chives, fennel, marjoram, mint, tarragon thyme, and winter savory. In addition to these practical considerations, give some thought to aesthetic ones. You don't have to make a plan as complex as an Elizabethan maze, but this is a good time to stretch your imagination. A circular or half-moon plot, for example, can be divided into wedges, or a large rectangular plot can feature free-form, stepping-stone-shaped clumps separated by narrow, meandering dirt walkways. You can also use colorful or especially verdant plants, such as purple basil and curly leaf parsley, as borders for your plot.

- **DON'T FERTILIZE:** Odd as it seems, almost all herbs do better in average or poor soil than in rich soil. In rich soil, herbs produce luxuriant foliage but the flavor will be poor. A few herbs such as chervil, fennel, and summer savory may require modest amounts of fertilizer from time to time but, aside from these, this is one garden routine you can more or less forget about.

- **SOW INDOORS, TRANSPLANT IN SPRING:** Most herbs can be sown from seed. They can also be purchased from plant stores and nurseries. If you want to grow from seed, it's best to start them indoors in the late winter and move outdoors when the weather warms in spring. Plant seeds in light, well-drained soil in shallow containers, and be careful not to cover seeds with too much soil. Most seedlings will transplant very well, with the exception of coriander, dill, and fennel, which don't like to be moved and should be sown outdoors.

- **PROVIDE WINTER PROTECTION:** Many herbs have shallow root systems that will heave up out of the ground during spring thaws. Because of this, it's advisable to provide winter protection for perennial herbs. Apply a four-inch-deep mulch of straw, oak leaves, or evergreen boughs after the ground freezes in early winter, and leave in place until plant growth begins in early spring.

ENJOYING YOUR HARVEST

Unlike fruits and vegetables, which take weeks or months to ripen, herbs can be enjoyed almost immediately. As soon as the plant has enough foliage to carry on growth, you can begin picking leaves from it. For good flavor, the best time of day to pick is mid-morning, after the dew has evaporated but before the sun becomes too strong. To dry herbs, pick leaves before buds open or, for seeds, pick seed heads before they begin to change from green to brown or gray. Wash leaves and seed heads in cold water and drain thoroughly, and place in shallow pans to dry. You can also dry leaves by hanging entire stems upside down and stripping the leaves off after they dry. Never store leaves or seeds before they are completely dry, as they will spoil.

ATTRACT BIRDS

You can make your garden a haven for birds simply by supplying them with the things they need most—food, fresh water, and shelter. Here are some tips:

- Birds like fresh water. Many birdbaths fail to attract birds because the water is often allowed to become stagnant. It is easier to maintain a shallow pan that can easily be emptied and cleaned.

- Birds are especially in need of water in early spring, when shallow pools and puddles freeze. A pan of warm water in their favorite drinking spot will draw them to your yard.

- Suet, wired to a tree limb or container, is a favorite winter food because it provides the caloric energy birds need to keep warm.

- Bright, freshly painted houses appeal to people but not to most birds. They don't want to sequester their young in a conspicuous place. Natural wood, infrequent painting, and somber colors work best.

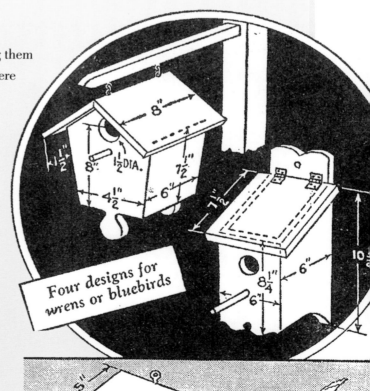

Four designs for wrens or bluebirds

- Nesting materials can be placed nearby—but not in—birdhouses. Strips of rag, string, and short pieces of raffia are popular.

- Make sure bird houses have some ventilation. A number of quarter-inch holes bored under the eves do the trick.

- With the exception of the purple martin, which enjoys sunny apartment living, birds want their own homes. Avoid large, multiple-nest dwellings.

- House wrens will nest almost anywhere, but be sure the entrance of the house you provide measures no more than seven-eighths of an inch, as the bird wants to feel secure from cats and sparrows.

- Robins prefer to build on sheltered shelves that are open on three sides. A simple board nailed under the eaves in a quiet spot will be enticing to them.

- Bluebirds are frequently driven from their homes by sparrows, but this can be prevented by providing the correct home for each. For bluebirds, put up

a swinging house and have it in place by mid-March. Offer sparrows, which will not nest in a swinging house, one that is fixed.

—adapted from *The Complete Book of Garden Magic*, 1935

MAKE YOUR OWN HUMMINGBIRD STATION

If you live in an area with hummingbirds, you're missing a treat if you don't attract these lively jewels-on-the-wing to your yard. Here's a quick, easy way to do it:

1. Select a small, wide-mouthed bottle (such as a medicine bottle) and paint it a bright flower color.

2. Using a six- to ten-inch piece of lightweight wire (florists' wire will do), loop the end of the wire around the neck of the bottle and attach the other end to a branch, pole, or flower box. The bottle should be tipped at a slight angle, about forty-five degrees, but need not be near a perch, as hummingbirds feed on the wing. Since the bird's natural food is flower pollen, a location near flowers is best.

PURPLE MARTIN
EACH NEST SPACE 6 X 6 X 6 IN. ENTRANCE 1 IN. ABOVE FLOOR & 2½ IN. DIAMETER. PLACE HOUSE 15 TO 20 FT ABOVE GROUND AND EQUALLY AS FAR FROM BUILDINGS AND TREES

DRAWER AND SECTION TYPES MAKE CLEANING EASY.

SHELF BRACKET SUPPORT

HOUSE WREN
NEST 6 TO 10 FT. ABOVE GROUND INSIDE SIZE 4 X 4 IN. BY 6 OR 8 IN. HIGH. ENTRANCE 1 TO 6 IN. ABOVE FLOOR. HOLE ⅞ IN. DIAMETER.

TIN CAN WREN HUT

HINGED FLOOR

SCREEN SUMMER HOUSE

SHELF FOR USE UNDER EAVES.

HOLE

BLUE BIRD
INSIDE SIZE 5 X 5 IN. BY 8 IN. DEEP ENTRANCE 6 IN. ABOVE FLOOR—HOLE 1½ IN. NESTS 5 TO 10 FT. ABOVE GROUND.

ROBIN
INSIDE SPACE 6 TO 8 IN. BY 8 IN. HIGH PLACE HOUSE 10 TO 15 FT ABOVE GROUND AND HAVE AT LEAST 3 SIDES OPEN.

3. Cut a piece of nylon or wire mesh to fit over the end of the bottle. This will keep bees and insects away from the food inside without posing a problem for the hummingbird, whose beak is narrow and needle-like.

4. Place food in the bottle. Honey works best, but sugar water is almost as good. Attach the mesh cap with a rubber band, string, or loop of florists' wire.

5. Refill the jar often, as these tiny creatures consume an astonishing amount of food.

BUILD A COLD FRAME

Avid gardeners often tire of buying seedlings and sets from nurseries and get the urge to nurture their own plants from seed. In many parts of the country, this isn't possible without a specialized structure. And, while most people don't have room for a greenhouse, many do have space for a cold frame. "In one season," wrote Winifred Hayward in *Better Homes & Gardens* in 1941, "my cold frame has paid for itself. Plus I've had the convenience of having everything at hand for planting and a good surplus of plants to replace those in the garden which, by accident or bugs, met an untimely end." She then went on to tell how it's done:

"Since cold frames should be in a sunny exposure and in a well-drained spot, my cold frame is built up against the south side of the house with the sash sloping toward the sun.

"I bought 3 sash 3 x 6 feet, made with overlapping glass panes to guard against rain dripping in. The three cost $7.50. Used bricks for the foundation cost $3, and the lumber used to make a slanting framework on which the sash rest cost $3. Total materials cost $13.50.

"Size of my cold frame was governed by the three sash placed alongside each other—6 feet x 9 feet. The soil below the frame was dug out to a depth of 3 feet. This was filled with a foot of coarse gravel, and on top of that, a foot of cinders. This gave me good drainage. Around the edge on the cinders I laid four double rows of bricks to insure a firm foundation.

"Inside the bricks on top of the cinders I poured a foot of coarse sand. This brought the bed up to ground level. (I use no loose soil in my cold frame.)

"Two more double rows of bricks were then added above ground, and a top row then set across the last double row to give a neat appearance. This wall, when finished, was 12 inches above ground level.

"I've seen a number of cold frames made entirely of wood, but they don't last as long and they don't hold the heat as well.

"In sections having cold winters, a poured-concrete base is preferable though not essential. It's heavier and tighter than brick, thus eliminating all cracks and retaining the maximum of heat.

The author and her $13.50 coldframe that gives her a head-start on spring

Hinged sash opened to show construction. Two light bulbs prevent freezing

Foundation details. Layers of sand, cinders, and gravel control moisture

A plan for an inexpensive, one-sash, wood coldframe set away from house

Another plan—using a lead-covered electric heating cable and thermostat

"On top of our brick foundation we made a wood frame in which the sash fit. It's higher in back so that the sash slants and thus carries off the rain and lets as much sunlight inside as possible. After giving the frame two coats of white paint, we hinged the sash on the back edge of the frame.

"To hold the sash up when open, we put a screw-eye in the edge of each. I have three tall posts available, each with several hooks screwed into it. Thus the screw-eye can be hooked into any of the hooks on the post and the sash kept open to any height desired.

"For heat we ran an electric cable outside and fitted up two electric bulbs inside. These bulbs are lighted when it's freezing outside, and in our Oklahoma climate they give just sufficient heat to keep the plants safe.

"A thermometer hanging inside tells me when to open or shut the sash.

"This method of heating wouldn't do for northern states. However, there are several electrical devices on the market for heating hotbeds to any temperature desired.

"Plants must have fresh air. Even in winter your cold frame can often be opened during the sunnier parts of the day, even just a little crack. I cover my frame on cold nights with old rugs."

—Winifred Hayward,
Better Homes & Gardens, March 1941

VENTILATING THE GARDEN FRAME

INDEX

BIBLIOGRAPHY

Biles, Roy E. *The Complete Book of Garden Magic*. Chicago: J. G. Ferguson, 1943.

Biles, Roy E. *Modern Family Garden Book*. Chicago: J. G. Ferguson, 1935.

Bush-Brown, Louise, and James Bush-Brown. *America's Garden Book*. New York: Charles Scribner's Sons, 1939.

McCurdy, Robert. *The Book of Garden Flowers*. New York: Sun Dial Press, 1937.

Popular Mechanics' Garden Book. Chicago: Popular Mechanics Press, 1942.

ABOUT THE AUTHOR

SUSAN WAGGONER is a writer of nonfiction and fiction books, including *Nightclub Nights: Art, Legend, and Style, 1920–1960* (Rizzoli, 2001) and *The Women's Sports Encyclopedia*. A native of Minnesota and an alumna of the Iowa Writer's Workshop, she currently lives in New York City.